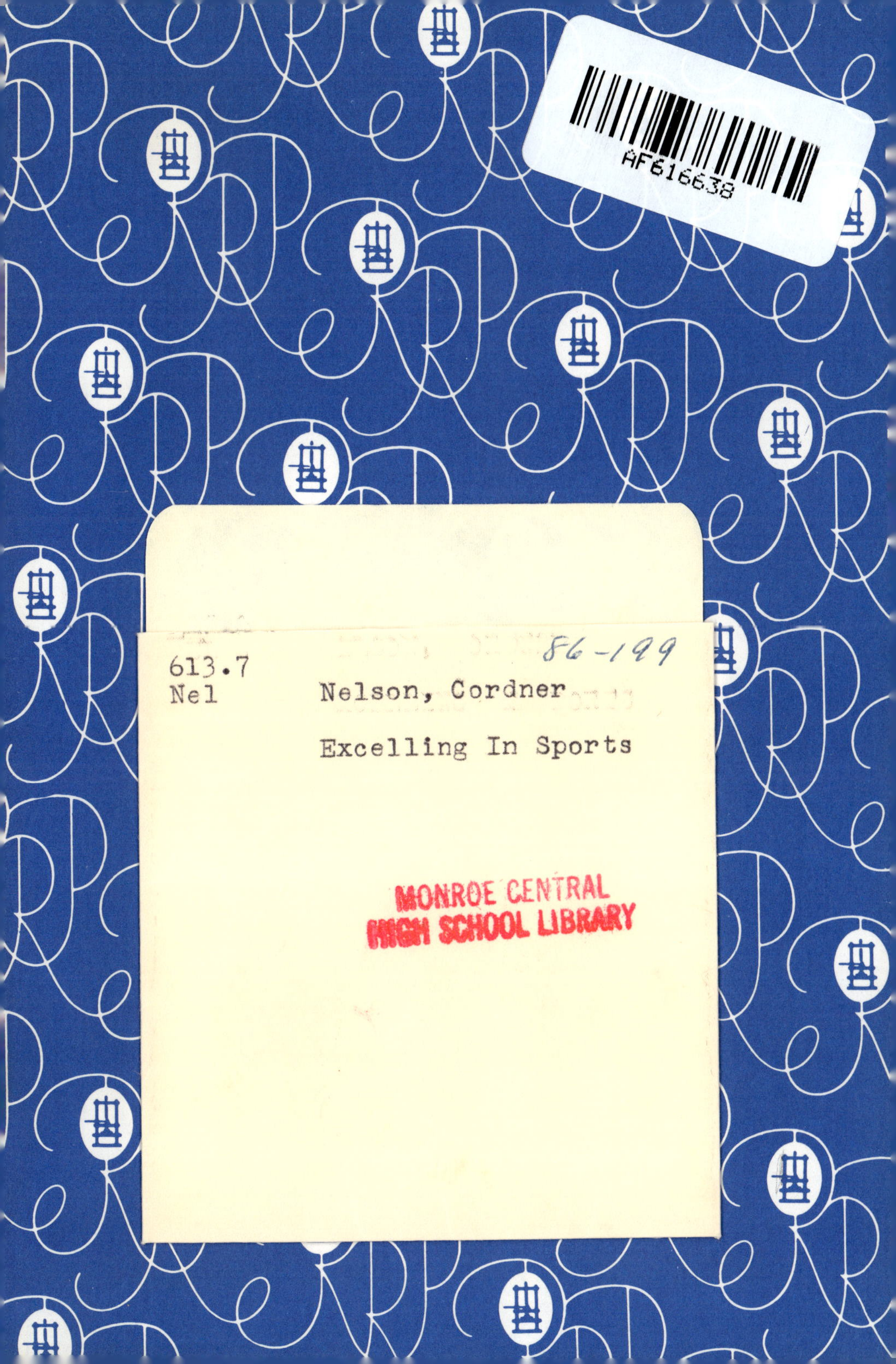
AF616638

Excelling

IN SPORTS

How to Train

by Cordner Nelson

THE ROSEN PUBLISHING GROUP
New York

Published in 1985 by The Rosen Publishing Group, Inc.
29 Eat 21st Street, New York, N.Y. 10010

First Edition

Library of Congress Cataloging in Publication Data

Nelson, Cordner.
Excelling in sports.

1. Physical education and training. I. Title.
GV341.4.N45 1984 613.7'07 84-18012
ISBN 0-8239-0631-0

Manufactured in the United States of America

About the Author

Cordner Nelson has been a sports enthusiast for fifty-eight years, as a competitor, fan, spectator, reporter, and student. In 1948, after five years of war service had sidetracked his plan to be a coach, he and his brother, Bert, founded *Track & Field News*, now the sport's leading English-language magazine.

In researching his 1967 best-selling biography, *The Jim Ryun Story*, Nelson became more aware of the amazing capacity for improvement in the human body. This concept found its way into his novel *The Miler* (1969) and two track histories, *Track and Field: The Great Ones* (1970) and *Runners & Races: 1500/Mile* (1973).

His key discovery came while making a thorough study of training methods during the writing of the *Runners' World Advanced Running Book.* He came to the startling conclusion that most athletes fail to train to their fullest capacity. Thus was born the idea for *How to Train.*

To Libby and David

Contents

Introduction

On September 7, 1962, in Wichita, Kansas, a tall, frail boy of fifteen with round shoulders and a soft face plodded hopelessly around the running track behind other members of East High School's cross-country team. Already a failure in other sports, he fell farther behind, and he floundered across the line in thirteenth place with a dismal mile time of 5:38.

Four years later the same boy flew in triumph to New York, where he stood in front of dozens of cameras and reporters to receive the Sullivan Award. He had received the largest vote in history for his glorious feat of breaking the world's records in the half-mile and mile, and several times his picture had been on the cover of national magazines and on national television. At the age of nineteen, he had become the most famous athlete in the world. His name was Jim Ryun.

Millions of people who want to do well in sports can find the secrets of that slim boy's fantastic progress in the three ingredients necessary for success. If you want to be a good athlete—as good as your natural ability allows—this book can help you succeed to an astonishing degree. Training is a science, and the principles you learn here can help you, whether you are a fourteen-year-old beginner or a thirty-year-old professional.

You need these three ingredients for success: natural ability, effort, and training.

Natural Ability

Nobody has a talent for everything, but everybody has a talent for something.

Like most boys, Jim Ryun wanted to be an athlete. He became a runner simply because he learned that he had natural talent. He had tried bowling and baseball with little but discouragement. He was too frail for football, too awkward for basketball, and he had failed to make the track team in junior high school. But he kept trying until he found a sport in which his undeveloped body had a chance to match his dreams.

A massive All-American tackle would have struggled in last in a cross-country race. A small man with the marvelous precision of a championship golfer would be wasted on a football team. With strenuous work, Jim Ryun might have made the basketball bench during his junior year of high school, but in a sport where he had aptitude he won the red-white-and-blue Olympic uniform.

Effort

Most successful athletes found a sport in which they had some ability, and then they *tried*. You can go a long way in this world if you try—in games or, even more important, in training. Few athletes ever tried harder than Jim Ryun. In his first full year of training he ran 4,380 miles, an average of 12 miles a day each and every day, in rain, snow, or Kansas heat.

How hard you try is *your* business. If you try hard enough you can develop your ability to an amazing degree. As long as you know that your success in developing your talent depends mostly upon how hard you try, you should be satisfied with whatever effort you put into it. Your effort will match your ambition.

Jim Ryun said it simply: "If a person is willing to work hard enough, it is possible to achieve a high goal."

Training

Part of trying—part of your effort to succeed—is in *how* you train. Therefore, correct guidance is the third ingredient you need.

Many athletes have reasonable capacity and try very hard but still fail because they do not practice in the right way. Golf courses are full of duffers who have tried for years but never break 90. Almost all of them have enough natural endowment to break 80, but they fail to train properly. They learned the wrong technique instead of a good swing.

One of the tragedies in the lives of thousands of young athletes is that they have no knowledge of the amazing capacity of their bodies. They like a sport for some reason, and so they try it—and sometimes they try hard—but they do not try in the right way; they do not realize the improvement they *could* make, and so they become discouraged and quit.

Billy Mills was almost an example of this. He went through an entire college career without notable success as a runner. He could have retired as an unknown, but he changed to a different type of training, moved up to a longer race, and won the 1964 Olympic 10,000 meters.

If you want to develop your capacities by trying, do it in the right way. Do not handicap yourself through ignorance. Learn how to train.

This book will lead you step by step through the whole process of training:

- I. How to plan your training
  - A. Examine your natural abilities
  - B. Select your sport
  - C. Make your training plan
  - D. Record your progress
- II. How to improve your talents
  - A. The principles of training
  - B. Strength
  - C. Speed and quickness
  - D. Endurance
  - E. Health
  - F. Training efficiency
- III. How to perfect new skills
  - A. How to learn technique
  - B. Practice

IV. Mental control
   A. Plans
   B. Emotional control
   C. Concentration

This book cannot change your natural abilities, and it cannot force you to try harder. It *can* tell you how to make certain your talents and efforts are not handicapped by ignorance.

CHAPTER • I

How to Plan Your Training

A. EXAMINE YOUR NATURAL ABILITIES

Once there was a fourteen-year-old boy who wanted to be a great runner. He read everything he could find about running. He watched track meets, he went out for the track and cross-country teams, he ran many miles a day during the off season, and he seldom thought of anything else he wanted so much.

After nine years of effort he knew he was only mediocre, he knew he lacked sufficient natural ability to be a good runner. With no effort at all, playing only occasionally for fun, he had proved himself to have more ability at basketball, tennis, golf, archery, badminton, Ping Pong, softball, and volleyball.

He was sorry he had worked so hard, "butting his head against a stone wall" while neglecting his real talents. But it was too late. His chance for a successful athletic career was gone.

This true story has happened to countless thousands of boys with slight variations. Most of them never know they could have had more success in another sport. They go through life believing that they lack athletic ability. Their entire future is slightly warped because of this false feeling of inferiority.

Not many people can be great champions, but most can learn one sport well enough to enjoy it and find satisfaction with a moderate degree of success. The main purpose of sport is not to achieve great success. Sports are desirable because they are fun, they promote health and good mental outlook, and they develop valuable traits of character. If you choose the right sport you can have all that in addition to your best chance for success.

Everybody should try as many sports as possible, for the experience. But before you begin to devote a large part of your time and energy toward success in one sport, make certain you do not lack one of the important natural aptitudes necessary for that particular sport.

Here are some of your natural attributes to consider:

• *Your height.* If you are not exceptionally tall, you should not set your heart on being a basketball center. Height is also an advantage in many other sports, but with the exception of basketball it is not as important as some other qualities.

Even in basketball a short man can be good, but he must have some other remarkable abilities. For every Bob Cousy there are thousands of would-be basketball players who fall by the wayside mainly because they are too short. Most of them are quick, agile, and accurate, and they could have used those talents with much success in several other sports.

On the other hand, many of the basketball players who stand 6′7″ tall are slower and more awkward than many athletes. The shorter you are in basketball, the more you need other abilities.

A very short man has an advantage in distance running. Many of the greatest runners have been only 5′5″ to 5′8″. Although 1969 AAU 6-mile champion Jack Bacheler is taller than 6′6″, he is a rare exception.

Shorter than average athletes are often quicker and more agile than taller men, and they are especially good as basketball infielders, skiers, divers, gymnasts, soccer players, hockey players, and in all the accuracy sports, especially tennis. In addition, short men have a place in sports with divisions based on weight, such as boxing, wrestling, and weight lifting.

If you are of average height the only sports you should eliminate—unless you have exceptional natural talent—are basketball and the weight events in track and field.

• *Your weight.* Strangely enough, your weight is less important in most sports than your height. That is because most athletes are fairly well proportioned and weight is a result of height. Also, your weight can be controlled to a large extent, whereas your height cannot.

The only sports in which weight is considered a necessity are football and the weight events of track and field, and even in those there are certain exceptions.

For example, not all football players need to be heavyweight. Many of the backfield men and some ends are built more for speed than for power. A shot-putter must be heavy and powerful, but javelin throwers can be light, and medium build will do for discus throwers, if they are tall. And, of course, boxers, wrestlers, and weight lifters come in all weights.

Even an occasional interior lineman in football makes news because he is relatively light, but you would be wise to cross "football lineman" off your list unless you are exceptionally big.

• *Your strength.* Most sports require a certain amount of strength, and added strength will give you an advantage, but you may be surprised how few sports require great natural strength.

As we will see later, you can develop your strength fairly easily, and that is enough for most sports.

Archery, for example, requires strength to bend a bow. The greater the "pull" of the bow, the faster it sends the arrow. The faster the arrow, the more accurate it is. Therefore, the strong archer has an advantage over the weaker archer. Most archers gradually develop strength over the years through bending their bows, but they can acquire much more strength rapidly by weight training. Therefore, you need not avoid archery if your natural strength is below average.

Some sports do require great natural strength. Unless you are unusually strong you should avoid weight lifting, wrestling, shot-putting, rowing, and football line play as your chosen sport. Special arm strength is needed to be a gymnast, baseball pitcher, boxer, swimmer, or javelin thrower. Cyclists require great leg strength.

You can test your strength in many ways, but none of them are very scientific. The best you can do in normal circumstances is to compare your strength with people of your own size and age in lifting, wrestling, Indian wrestling, gripping, pull-ups, push-ups, and shot-putting. You can test your throwing strength simply by throwing for distance.

• *Your speed.* There are really two kinds of speed. You can be quick of movement and yet not have great running speed. That is because your running speed is a combination of quickness, strength, and running form. For these purposes, consider running speed as separate from quickness.

Running speed is necessary only in the few sports that require running. You can improve your speed a little by training, but only about 10 percent as compared to 300 percent or more for strength. Therefore, the sports that require high-speed runners are open to you only if you have exceptional natural speed.

If you lack speed, you cannot be a sprinter or long jumper, and you have little chance in some of the football positions. Speed adds to your value in soccer, baseball, basketball, tennis, the pole vault and triple jump, middle-distance running, and in the other football positions.

The easiest way to test your speed is to run sprint races against opponents of your own age. If you are faster than about 90 percent of them, you have good speed.

• *Your quickness.* On the other hand, quickness of movement is important in many sports. It is probably the single most important talent you can have. Only a few sports do not place a premium on how fast you can make the movements.

You can succeed in a few sports without quickness. These include the accuracy sports such as archery, billiards, bowling, shuffleboard, and golf, although you do need quickness to hit a long ball in golf. Other sports requiring little quickness are weight lifting, distance running, rowing, and certain parts of gymnastics and diving.

You can test your quickness in general by trying some of the sports, especially basketball, boxing, and table tennis. Usually, the quickest people are the ones who make all their movements fast, even in daily living, although that is not a sure test.

If you want to go to the trouble and have some fun at the same time, you can test yourself and others for quickness of reaction.

Many expensive devices can be purchased, but you can make one that will do. You need a piece of board about 1 1/2 feet long. You need something like a spear—a knife or a stick with a nail in the end of it. And you need a table with a cover to protect it from damage.

The test is simple. Place the table close enough to a wall so the board will slide between with about 1/8 inch to spare. Another person holds the board so that the point of your "spear" is an inch from the board, exactly opposite a starting mark near the bottom of the board. When you are ready, the other person lets the board drop. When you see it begin to fall, you stop it as fast as possible by jamming the point of your spear into it. Your reaction time is measured by the distance the board drops before you can stop it. Marks on the board 1/4 inch apart will make it easy to measure. If you can stop the board in a shorter distance than other people, you are quicker than they are. It makes an interesting contest, comparing your reaction time with others'.

• *Your agility.* If you are awkward and poorly coordinated you should avoid most of the sports that require quick and accurate movements. In general, agility is needed in the same sports as quickness except for golf, swimming, cycling, and running. Two sports requiring exceptional agility instead of quickness are gymnastics and diving.

In some sports, agility depends upon your position. For example, if you have certain aptitudes you can get by without special agility if you are a football lineman, baseball slugger, or basketball center.

If you are exceptionally agile and have the other necessary natural gifts you might become a baseball shortstop, a basketball playmaker, a boxer, wrestler, hockey goalie, tennis player, high jumper, or pole vaulter.

There is no way to test your agility except by competing. If you can learn complicated movements quickly and easily compared with others, you are agile. A nonsports test might be how fast you learn such things as dancing, typing, or roller skating.

• *Your accuracy.* Some people are naturally more accurate than others, and they have a great advantage in the accuracy sports such as archery, billiards, bowling, shuffleboard, golf, and basketball. Accuracy is also important in tennis and badminton. Accuracy is what makes good baseball pitchers and football passers, and it is important in fencing, hockey, and soccer.

If you have this natural talent you can discover it easily. Any game in which you try to hit a target will enable you to compare your accuracy with others. You can throw darts, rocks, or baseballs. You can shoot baskets, throw a football, putt a golf ball, bowl, or play shuffleboard, marbles, or pool.

• *Your endurance.* Almost all sports require some endurance, but it is usually acquired simply by playing the game. Some sports, however, require extra ability to last. Although you can train yourself for endurance, certain sports require exceptional natural stamina.

For example, unless you have more than your share of natural energy you cannot be a good distance runner. Other endurance sports are cycling, rowing, long swimming races, and cross-country skiing.

In some sports you cannot be good without special endurance. In soccer, for instance, you must play continually. Your chances to rest are also limited in boxing, wrestling, and handball.

Stamina will make you more valuable in basketball, hockey, football, tennis, and water polo because when fatigue sets in your coordination suffers.

To test your endurance, keep in mind the fact that you want to test the energy that comes from a well-developed cardiovascular system—your heart and blood vessels. Holding your arms out for as long as possible is a test of muscular stamina only. The best way to test your cardiovascular endurance is to compare yourself with others in some activity at which you have had enough experience to develop a little skill. Walking is one. Running is better, if you have done any running. If you can jog for ten miles while most of your contemporaries cannot, you have better than average endurance.

It will do you no good to test your endurance at, for example, rowing unless you have practiced the movements, because then it becomes a test of muscular stamina.

• *Your adaptability.* Some people can adjust to new situations much more easily than others. If you lack this ability you will always be a jump behind in lively ball games as well as in combat sports such as boxing, wrestling, and fencing.

You cannot test yourself for adaptation. You can only observe or have someone else observe you. Analyze your attitudes. Do you prefer golf over tennis because the golf ball stands still for you, or do you prefer tennis because of the challenge presented by the moving ball? Do you prefer contests in which you test yourself against your previous records, as in golf, track, bowling, and gymnastics; or would you rather compete against an individual whose moves you must counteract, as in boxing, basketball, and water polo?

• *Your cooperation.* If you choose a team sport you must be able to cooperate. That means that you must sometimes sacrifice your own glory for the good of the team. If you do not like that idea, try a more individual sport.

If you give yourself a grade—high, average, or low—for each of these natural abilities, you can make a list of the best sports for you. Compare your abilities with this checklist:

Checklist of Abilities Needed in Sports

(X = necessary for this sport; + = valuable to part of this sport)

	Height	*Weight*	*Strength*	*Speed*	*Quickness*	*Endurance*	*Agility*	*Accuracy*	*Adaptation*	*Cooperation*
Archery								X		
Badminton					X		X			
Baseball				+	+		+	+		
Basketball	X				X	+	X	X	X	X
Billiards								X		
Bowling								X		
Boxing					X	X	X		X	
Diving							X			
Fencing					X	+	X		X	
Football		X	X	+	+		+	+	X	X
Golf								X		
Gymnastics			+				X			
Handball					X		X		X	
Hockey					X	X	X	+	X	X
Horseshoes (also Darts, Shuffleboard)									X	
Rowing			X			X				
Skiing						+	X			
Soccer			X			X				X
Speed Skating				+		+				
Swimming			+		+	X				
Table Tennis					X		X		X	
Tennis					X	+	X	X	X	+
Track & Field	+	+	X	X	+	X	+			
Volleyball	+				X		X		+	+
Water Polo			+		+	+		+	X	X
Weight lifting	X									
Wrestling	X				X		X		X	

B. SELECT YOUR SPORT

Before you attempt to match your talents to a sport, you should consider the situation in which you find yourself and your purposes in playing athletic games.

• Your physical situation includes your age, health, previous experience, and natural ability. You have already thought about your talents, and you should work toward perfect health at all times. Any previous experience in sports should help you decide.

Special consideration should be given to your age. If you are forty years old you should not take up sports such as football, boxing, sprinting, or hockey. On the other hand, it is almost never too late to take up the accuracy sports such as archery, billiards, bowling, and golf. If you are only nine years old, or fourteen, you have a choice of the entire list of sports and should try as many as possible, because if you never try one you may miss out on something good.

• Your available time and energy. How much free time do you have to devote to a sport? If you have only an hour a day, you should stick to one sport, because an hour is hardly enough time even for one. If you have little time to spare, try one of the uncomplicated sports, such as running or cycling, instead of those that require many hours of practice, such as golf, tennis, boxing, basketball, fencing, swimming, or pole vaulting. Even if you have a lot of time, you must choose between some sports that share the same season, such as baseball and track.

• Your available facilities. If you live in a small town without a football team, you can forget about football. In most areas there is no ice hockey team, and many of the other sports are neglected. To learn a team sport, you need a team. To do it alone requires so much time, effort, and talent that the odds against you are far too high.

Obviously, you can eliminate snow sports when no snow is available. The same applies to many other sports: You need gymnasium facilities for many, and athletic fields for some.

On the other hand, if you believe you have talent for a certain sport but lack facilities, do not give up entirely. You may have the facilities later, in high school or college. In the meantime, you can do many things that will help you prepare for that sport.

• Your desire to work. If you do not want to work very hard at sports, your best bet is to take up the most convenient sports, usually in season, and enjoy as many as possible. But if your ambition is to be as good as your natural ability allows, you must put in thousands of hours of work. Many high school boys train four hours a day.

It is not the number of hours you train that spells success so much as the quality of your training. To work hard does not always mean to tire yourself out. It can mean to concentrate hard for long periods of time. You might enjoy four hours of practice at golf, bowling, archery, or even some of the more tiring sports.

As a general rule of thumb, the sports that require much endurance are the ones that require hard, fatiguing work. If you do not like hard work, avoid those sports.

Why Compete?

After you have thought about your situation, including your talents, you should think about your purpose in trying a sport. Here are some of the main reasons people compete in sports:

• Movement is a natural desire. All animals, including human beings, enjoy movement. Children, puppies, and colts do a lot of running around for the sheer pleasure of it. This feeling of speed, power, and freedom is part of the joy you get from sports.

Ron Clarke, when he was the fastest distance runner of all time, said, "I thoroughly enjoy running 100-odd miles a week. If I didn't, I wouldn't do it."

• Play movements are even more fun. Everybody likes to play. It is fun to shoot baskets, hit a ball, jump as far as you can, dive cleanly into the water, and otherwise enjoy the stylized movements within the rules of sports. This fun can continue for most of your life if you choose one of the many sports suitable to middle-aged people.

• Trying is important. As soon as most people try to do

something, they want to do it *well.* It is part of human nature, and the striving leads to a desire to do it better than other people. The English philosopher Bertrand Russell said:

"Consistent purpose is not enough to make life happy, but it is an almost indispensable condition of the happy life."

If you want to *try*, this book will help you.

• Exercise promotes health. Many young people are not concerned with good health because they are naturally healthy and think it will last forever. It is most important for your health that you exercise regularly, and it is particularly important when you are young because of your excess energy.

Even while you are young, exercise helps you have better posture, clearer skin, a more vibrant appearance, and the wonderful feeling of energy.

• Sports bring friends. You will meet more people and find more common interests among fellow athletes because of sports. The desire to have friends is one of the strongest emotions people feel. Sports create a bond based on common interests and respect, and that fulfills your need to belong.

• Sports can bring in money. An athlete who is good enough at his sport can become a professional, and some of them earn large sums of money. Others use their knowledge and interest in other ways, such as coaching.

• Sports build character. Even if you do not become a champion or an All-American, if you have developed your talents fully you will feel a satisfaction with yourself beyond anything felt by people who never try.

People who merely drift through life believe they are victims of fate, or of their inherited tendencies, or of their parents or society. They usually blame their troubles on somebody else.

People who try, on the other hand, believe they can help shape society. They believe in trying to control their lives, to make changes, to improve themselves. They are waging their own personal war on the degenerative forces of a society bent on comfort at the expense of health, self-discipline, and self-reliance.

There is no stronger character builder than self-imposed discipline, and that is what you do when you train for sports. Training, applied gradually, lets you accept more and more self-discipline. As a result, you are quite willing to do what is right, for yourself and for society, and you will like yourself. Your ego is your own thing, and you are the judge of what satisfies it.

Now you can think about matching your own talents and situation with your purposes for wanting to be an athlete. You are the only person in the world who can do this, but you can do it right only if you think clearly and do not let yourself be swayed by emotions and preconceived ideas.

If you are already dreaming about being a great quarterback, the sooner you put it out of your mind and face reality the better off you will be—unless you have all the rare qualities needed.

When you judge your talents, consider yourself average in each one until you learn that you are either lacking that talent or have a special ability.

List all the sports you think might interest you, whether because of glamor or because of your purposes. Next to each sport, show your special talents. Then show any lack that will hurt you in that sport.

That much effort, with some thinking, should cut your list of possible sports to one or a very few. Many athletes compete in more than one sport, especially while they are in high school. The younger you are, the more variety you should try. Give yourself a chance to find your best sport.

C. MAKE YOUR TRAINING PLAN

Most people make a mistake when they first take up a sport. They want to play, to have fun. They do not want to waste time and energy on unpleasant training, so they do it the easy way—or so they think.

Actually, they are doing it the hard way. Every skill you learn with incorrect form is much harder to correct than if you learn correctly in the first place. Most people who learn a skill improperly never relearn it. That is why you see so many odd styles, even among professionals—at bat, on the basketball and tennis courts, on the golf course, at the high-jump pit.

If you begin by learning the fundamentals correctly, you will not have quite as much fun in the first few weeks, but from then on you will have much more fun than if you have a constant struggle against faulty form.

Therefore, the best way to start in a sport is to decide what you need to learn and then learn it systematically. If you do, you will be far better a year from now than if you rush right in and begin playing.

To understand how to make a training plan you must consider what is needed in your sport:

Strength

Many athletes do no strength training at all. Whatever strength they develop comes from the demands of their sport. That is bad, because everybody should do enough strength training to reach general fitness, and a basic muscular weakness can cause a fault in your form.

For example, leg strength might appear to have no part in your golf swing, but weak legs can cost you a little power, especially after two or three hours of walking around the course. This benefit cannot be proven, but it is better to waste a little energy than to give away part of your potential.

On the theory that a generally strong body cannot hurt you and probably does some good on a fundamental level, you should have *minimum* general strength for any sport you try.

Certain sports obviously require more general strength than others. As a rule of thumb, the more intensively you move and the more of your body you use, the more general strength training you need.

Thus, you should have *maximum* general strength for football, boxing, wrestling, and perhaps water polo and hockey because they all require your full body in man-to-man contact of a violent nature. Maximum general strength is also needed for a foundation in any sport in which you must build great special strength, such as weight lifting or shot-putting.

Medium general strength should be enough for most other sports, and the accuracy sports that do not require violent movements need only minimum general strength.

For the first step in your training plan for each sport, write down, "General strength" and add either "minimum," "medium," or "maximum."

Next you must consider special strength. Each sport has different movements. You can perform some of these movements much better if you have great strength. Examples are pulling the bow in archery, lifting your entire body with your arms in gymnastics, forcing back opposing linemen in football, turning over a wrestler, lifting a heavy weight overhead, and putting a 16-pound shot as far as you can.

Other movements require great speed, and a stronger muscle can move a weight—such as a bat or your whole body—faster than a weak muscle. Examples where strength is needed to improve speed include swinging a bat or racket, throwing a ball, sprinting, swimming, skating, and throwing a punch.

Think about the movements you must make in your sport. You can improve in most of those movements if you are stronger in the muscles you use. Therefore, you should do special strength training for your particular movements.

If you are a high jumper or a basketball player you want to improve your spring so you can jump higher. An archer has no use for leg spring, but he needs strength to pull 60 to 90 pounds back to his ear and hold it perfectly still without trembling. That strength is of no use to a quarterback; when he takes the football back to his ear there is no resistance; but when he throws a long pass he needs the strength to make his arm move fast.

Go through each of your movements in slow motion and think about where extra strength will help improve that movement. Then write on your training plan, "Special strength" and list each of those movements.

It is important to develop these strengths early in your training, because strength influences your form. Whenever your strength improves you are capable of doing something you could not do before, so if your strength is constantly changing, your form must also change.

Speed and Quickness

Unlike strength, speed is difficult to improve. A 100-yard-dash man, for example, usually considers himself lucky if he can improve his speed 2 percent in a season. Clyde Jeffrey, who later equaled the world record at 9.4, began sprinting in February of his junior year in high school. In his first time trial he ran 10.5; then he spent the whole season trying to run 10.1. More mature sprinters often improve only one-tenth of a second in a year.

On the other hand, the slower you are to start with, the more improvement you can make. Jeffrey had good sprinting form from the beginning, whereas most people have a lot to learn. Also, the biggest improvement in sprinting can be made in the first few yards. Thus, your speed in other running sports—such as football, basketball, tennis, and baseball—is for shorter distances, so your percentage of improvement can be much higher.

For example, if a 100-yard sprinter learns to get off the blocks one yard faster and to gain one yard in his pickup over the first ten yards, he is two yards faster. At 100 yards that is only a 2 percent improvement, but in ten yards it is a 20 percent improvement. Anyone except a few natural wonders can improve 20 percent in ten yards, and that is extremely useful.

Quickness of movement seems entirely different from your running speed, but it is really the same. You can learn quickness in exactly the same way you learn a sprint start.

Make a list of all your movements that require speed or quickness. An improvement of one-hundredth of a second can make the difference between mediocrity and excellence. In boxing, for example, it can make the difference between being knocked out and feeling a cool breeze as a glove swishes past your face.

Endurance

Like strength, your endurance can be improved greatly, but some sports require more endurance than others. You should do a minimum amount of general endurance training for your health alone.

In addition to your health, you can improve your skill in the late stages of a game by having more endurance. When you begin to tire, your coordination begins to fail. Thus, near the end of an important game, the athlete who "chokes" may really be fatigued to the point where he cannot go on.

As we shall see when we study endurance, it can be divided into general endurance and special endurance. Everyone should do the minimum general endurance training, but some sports require more.

Certain sports are primarily endurance sports—distance running and swimming, cycling, rowing, and cross-country skiing. Other sports require such continuous action that you must have maximum endurance to compete. Those include soccer, hockey, boxing, and wrestling.

Sports that permit you to rest in between action—such as football, basketball, tennis, and handball—require much general endurance, but not the maximum.

In your plan, after "General endurance" write "minimum," "medium," or "maximum" for each of your sports.

Special endurance is the ability of one muscle group to continue for long periods without undue fatigue. You may have great general endurance but poor special endurance for certain activities. A good distance runner, for example, could not swim well unless he developed special endurance in his swimming muscles.

Practice and participation in your sport take care of most of the special endurance you need, but when a particular burden is placed on one group of muscles you want to be certain you have some reserve strength. That applies to a pitcher's arm, an archer's pull, a basketball player's spring, a boxer's punch, a tennis player's serve, a cyclist's legs, and a rower's arms.

Make a list of your movements that must stand the strain of long, continued action.

Skills

Unlike strength, speed, and endurance, which are needed in almost all sports, each skill you learn is good for only one sport. (Note: Running fast is a skill, but it is considered under speed. The only other exception is swimming, which is also used in water polo.)

At first you might think your sport has only a few skills you must learn, and in some sports that is true. Distance running, for example, requires mainly economy of effort in running form plus skill in judging pace.

But tennis requires innumerable skills. The forehand drive alone—not considering chips and slices or backhands, volleys, lob volleys, and other strokes—requires many skills. Some players are very skillful at hitting a drive when the ball is waist high but cannot hit it shoulder high, or knee high, or on the run, or if it is too fast or too slow. Then there are skills involved in *where* you hit it—down the line requires a different stroke from crosscourt—and how fast you hit it, and how much top spin you put on it. A tennis player may try a thousand different combinations in a week.

Your job now, at this stage of preparing your training schedule, is to list all the skills you want to learn in your sport. That will take some thinking, but it will be good for you. Don't worry about missing a few skills; you will think of them later.

The point of this exercise is to make you aware of all the complexities of your sport. It is never as simple as it seems. For example, many people think driving a golf ball is only one skill. But hitting the ball straight is one skill and hitting it a long distance is another, and they do not always go together. Add the skill of being able to control a small slice, like Ben Hogan, or a small hook, or to hit it high to take advantage of a strong tail wind or low into a strong head wind, and you begin to realize that several skills are involved in one seemingly simple act.

Thinking about each part of your sport is the beginning of learning those skills, as we shall see later. For now, make a list of every skill you can use in your sport.

Now you have a list of all the things you must learn. Next you must plan how to learn them. That is discussed in detail in the two main sections of the book, How to Improve Your Talents and How to Learn New Skills. As you learn how to train for each one, list it on your training plan.

Your third step is to make a training schedule. That varies for each sport, of course, and it varies according to how much time you want to spend. If you intend to train two hours a day almost every day of the year, your schedule will be much different from one in which you train five days a week for the season of that particular sport.

No matter what your sport, you can start training for strength, speed, and endurance. Whether you are aiming for the minimum, medium, or maximum level, you begin in the same way.

At the same time you want to start learning the skills of your sport.

This requires careful attention to planning, and you should not begin until you understand the principles.

D. RECORD YOUR PROGRESS

As soon as you start training, keep a record of it.

A diary or log of all your training is invaluable for future study as well as being of interest in later years. Possibly its greatest value, however, is to make a running comparison of how your actual training is progressing compared with your plan. It can help you check up on yourself.

Your training diary can be a simple record in a looseleaf binder or in a bound notebook. You can write anything you want, but here are a few suggestions:

• Date, time of day, and length of workout.

• Environmental conditions, such as temperature, wind, rain, humidity, snow, or anything else that affects training.

• Personal conditions, such as your weight before and after, pulse rate, hours of sleep, any change in food, illness, injuries.

• Subjective feelings about your performance, such as how eager you were to work out, how tired you were, and how confident you felt about your skills.

• Your actual workout, in detail. Include what you did to learn or practice each skill. This is the place to make notes of anything you learned so that you can study it in the future.

• Results of competition or training tests. If you play a game of handball, even for fun, analyze your performance. Note any skill that worked better or worse than you think it should and try to determine why. Underline important points you might want to find in the future. This is also a place to keep a record of your opponents.

• General subjective thoughts about your progress in keeping up with your training plan. This is something like baring your conscience, or confession. If you have neglected some part of your training, write it down and write down what you intend to do about it.

The main purpose of your training diary is to help you improve, and it *will* help—if you use it.

CHAPTER • II

How To Improve Your Talents

A. THE PRINCIPLES OF TRAINING

In general, your body improves in two ways. One is in learning new skills, and that is discussed in the next section. The other is by changing itself in order to meet the demands you put upon it.

To understand this, you must first understand "stimulus and response." A stimulus is something that causes a living thing to react; the response to that stimulus is the reaction. For example, if you accidentally touch something hot, that is a stimulus. Your reaction is to jerk your hand away; that is a response. Stimulus and response are used together; one causes the other.

Everything you do is the result of stimulus-response mechanisms. Some are automatic and beyond your control, such as the beating of your heart, the flow of your digestive juices, and reflexes such as your knee-jerk or the blinking of your eyes. You could not live without these automatic responses.

Other responses are the result of your own decision. For example, you can make your hand jerk back as if you had burned a finger. This is the kind of response you stimulate when you develop a skill. But for now you must know about responses that are automatic.

You might ask, "Why do I want to know about something I cannot control?"

The answer is "You *can* control it. Your response is automatic, all right, and beyond your control, but you can control the *stimulus*."

Consequently, if you want a muscle to become stronger you cannot make it react by an effort of your will, but you can stimulate it so that it will strengthen itself. You do that very simply, merely by using the muscle.

In this way, all training is no more than a series of controlled stimulus-response units. In some you can control your response, and that is how you learn skills (discussed in the next section of the book). In others, you can control the stimulus, and that is how you improve your natural strength and endurance. Therefore, in this section we shall see how you can stimulate your body into making the improvements you want.

First you must understand one more word—*stress*. A stress is a stimulus that is strong enough to put your body out of balance. Heat is a stress, and your body responds by sweating. Cold is a stress, and you respond with "goose pimples." Actually, the responses of your body are more complicated than that, because whenever your normal balance is upset, your body goes through many actions to restore balance.

Incidentally, the actions that go on within your body make for fascinating reading. Nothing in the world is so complicated and remarkable as your body, and you cannot help but enjoy learning more about it. At the same time, such knowledge can only improve your ability to control your physical condition.

Detailed physiology is outside the scope of this book. It is enough to know that if a stimulus is strong enough—if it is a stress—your body will react to it in certain definite ways.

When you were a baby, learning to walk, a few steps could be called a stress. Now you can walk around for a few minutes without upsetting your internal physiology at all. Walking at a normal pace is so easy that it cannot be called a stress unless you keep it up for a long time.

That means you must know how much stress to use in stimulating your body during training. The whole art and science of physical conditioning depends upon the amount of stress you give yourself.

The most famous investigator of stress was the late Dr. Hans Selye of Canada. His theories about stress are included in his General Adaptation Syndrome. (A syndrome is a group of symptoms, as in a disease. Adaptation is another word for "response".)

According to Dr. Selye, the body reacts to stress in three stages: the Alarm Reaction, the Stage of Resistance, and the Stage of Exhaustion. Each is important.

The Alarm Reaction is divided into shock and countershock. Shock is the first reaction. A weak stress causes little obvious shock, but a strong stress can cause anything from a frantic pounding of the heart to small ulcers in the stomach and intestines. The body is now out of balance.

The countershock is the body's fight to correct that imbalance. First, messengers called hormones rush through the blood to various parts of the body and start an amazing series of reactions. Some of the most common reactions are faster heartbeat, faster breathing, increased sugar in the blood for use as fuel for the muscles, higher blood pressure for a more efficient blood supply to the muscles, and shutting off of blood to the stomach and other parts of the body that do not need blood during this emergency.

The Stage of Resistance is what the body does if the stress continues or is repeated over and over again. During this stage, the wonderful mechanisms of the body adjust to the stress, repair any damages, and actually overcompensate by building more resistance than is needed for that stress.

For example, a slight friction on the skin, repeated over and over, will produce a callus that will protect the skin from greater friction. Vaccination with a small dose of smallpox serum will make one immune to the full terror of the disease. A broken arm will heal so well that it will probably never break there again.

As you have probably guessed, this Stage of Resistance is the one you use for your training. You simply stress yourself properly and your body overcompensates so that you can stand an even greater stress.

Unless the stress is too severe, and if you eat the proper raw materials for rebuilding, you can continue to adapt progressively for many years.

The third stage of stress is called the Stage of Exhaustion. According to Dr. Selye, you have only so much adaptive energy. When that is used up, your adaptation mechanism becomes overloaded and collapses.

Then you are in trouble, because you have no reserves left. Too much stress in training or competition can damage the body. Severe stress can result in prolonged shock and even death. When you reach the stage of failing adaptation, you must rest and restore your adaptive energy.

Thus, the secret of training is to remain in the second stage, the Stage of Resistance. If you do not reach it, you are not training. If you go too far, you are tearing yourself down. Obviously though, you improve faster if you are in the upper part of the Stage of Resistance, fairly close to the Stage of Exhaustion.

Your problem, then, is to recognize the signs of approaching exhaustion of your adaptive energies. Here are some of the warnings:

- Mental staleness. You feel tired often. You lose enthusiasm for training and competing. You lose your temper easily. You lose your appetite.
- Physical staleness. You may have aches and pains in your joints and muscles. Relaxing and sleeping may become difficult. You may have stomach upsets or a stuffy nose. You may sigh, tremble, and look pale. You may have hives on your skin or swollen lymph glands in your groin. You are easily injured.
- Physical symptoms you can check: You lose weight. Your resting pulse rate increases. You cannot do as well in training or competition.
- Physical symptoms checked by a doctor: Your blood pressure goes down, as do your red corpuscle count and your hemo-

globin values. Experienced sports medicine experts can detect overtraining with an electrocardiograph or heartometer.

You must train hard to make progress, but you must ease off if you suspect that you are approaching the level of failing adaptation. That requires patience and the knowledge that you *will* improve. Training that is too severe for you now will be too easy a year from now. The secret is to increase your training stress gradually.

B. STRENGTH

Increasing strength is both easy and important.

Strength is important in several ways:

- In some sports you cannot succeed without great general strength.
- Most sports require special strength in some part of the body.
- You will benefit from some general strength in all sports. In fact, you will benefit in all your activities. One example should convince you. All your weight, above your legs, is borne by your spinal column, and your spine cannot remain upright without the support of your trunk muscles. Weak trunk muscles lead to fatigue, which causes poor form and loss of efficiency. This could happen to you even in billiards or shuffleboard.

A strong muscle means more endurance, if all else is equal. That is because a strong muscle needs less energy to do the same amount of work as a weaker muscle.

A strong muscle gives you more speed because it can do more work with the same amount of energy.

A minimum amount of general strength training should be done by everyone. You can increase that amount for sports that require more strength. Whatever your requirements, you can train for strength by five different methods.

1. Exercises

Exercises include calisthenics and gymnastics, and they are also used for stretching, flexibility, and warmups.

As an example of an exercise, stand with your feet apart, arms outstretched. Twist your body to one side and bend until one hand touches the opposite knee. Doing a few of these might serve as part of a warmup. If you stretch a little, perhaps far enough to touch your ankle each time, you can call it a stretching exercise. If you gradually force yourself to touch lower and lower, you can call it a flexibility exercise. It has great benefits, but it does not increase your strength very much.

To understand how to increase strength you should understand a little about muscles, those remarkable machines that make your body move. Before you can move, a nerve impulse must reach a muscle. This can be under your control, or it can be a reflex response. A complicated chemical process takes place, and the muscle shortens.

If you want to close your fingers gently around an egg to keep it from falling, electrical impulses contract the muscles of your fingers enough to hold the egg. But if you contract your finger muscles as much as possible you will crush the egg.

This control you have over the amount of contraction in a muscle is possible because each muscle is made up of thousands of individual muscle fibers in groups of 100 to 150. Each group is stimulated by a single motor nerve. The more power you want, the more groups are used. The rapidity of the impulses through your motor nerves helps control the power of your muscles.

Physiologists disagree as to exactly what happens to increase the strength of muscle fibers, but everybody knows that if you contract a muscle against some resistance a few times, it becomes stronger. (Resistance is anything that makes it harder for you contract a muscle.)

This explains why the flexibility exercise described above does not increase strength very much: There is too little resistance.

Some exercises do provide resistance, however, and they can be used to increase strength. Any exercise in which you must lift all or part of your body provides enough resistance to build strength. Examples are pull-ups or push-ups from parallel bars.

But your strength increase is limited by your body weight. Once you become strong enough to do push-ups easily, the number you can do becomes more a matter of endurance than strength. To increase your strength even more, you must find a way to use more resistance.

Exercises, then, are limited in the amount they can increase strength. If your goal is only the minimum level of strength, exercises can usually do the job, and that is where most people should stop, with push-ups and pull-ups.

Exercises are particularly useful for strengthening the important trunk muscles that support the spine. Here are exercises that have been proved best for strengthening the abdominal muscles:

- Hang from a bar, lift your knees above your waist, and tilt your pelvis up for a few seconds.
- Sit in the same V-position and try to flatten your lower back against the mat.
- Lie on your side with your lower legs held. Twist your trunk and raise slowly to a vertical position.
- Lie on your back with hands behind your head, knees bent, feet held. Sit up and altrnately touch a knee with the opposite elbow.
- Kneel and lean far back. Hold for a few seconds before rcturning slowly to your upright position.

If you do each of these exercises a few times every day, you will reach the minimum strength level for your abdominal muscles. (If your sport calls for more than minimum strength, you can add dumbbells to these exercises.)

Exercises can strengthen other parts of the body. A few push-ups and pull-ups each day will maintain muscle tone in the arms and shoulders. But most exercises are an inefficient way to increase strength, because of the low resistance available to you.

One common exercise that you should avoid is deep knee bending. This causes a stretching of the knee ligaments, a weakness that makes injury easy. One tennis player did deep knee bends as part of his morning exercises every day for two years, and every day he felt a sharp pain in a line across each knee cap. Then he read about football trainers giving up that exercise, and he did so. Within two weeks he had no more knee pains.

That brings up an important point. Strength training involves strain. If, in any type of strength training, you feel pain, discontinue that activity or reduce it until the pain disappears. Begin again and gradually increase, at a slower rate, as long as the pain does not return.

2. **Isometrics**

An isometric contraction takes place when you exert muscular power against an unmoving object. If you try to lift a piano and it does not move, your muscular contraction is isometric. If the piano moves, your contraction is called isotonic. Your muscle remains the same during an isometric contraction. During an isotonic contraction your muscle changes length.

Many claims have been made for isometrics. For a while, most people believed you could obtain maximum strength by doing a few seconds of isometrics every day. That has proved to be far from the truth.

You can increase strength with isometrics, but there are many drawbacks:

- If a muscle is already strong, it gains little.
- You develop strength in only one position. For example, if you are trying to strengthen your leg drive for football and you push as hard as you can with your leg partially bent, you can strengthen it for that one position only. You need full strength through the full range of your leg's movement. Isometrics fail to develop flexibility.
- When the muscle does not move, far less endurance is developed.

• Isometrics require an extreme effort, but nothing moves, so you have no feeling of accomplishment.

Injuries can result from such extreme effort.

On the other hand, isometrics can help you add to your strength, especially when you lack time or equipment. For example, you can strengthen your grip or suck in your abdominal muscles while sitting in a car or in class.

3. **Resistance Training**

This is the term for an odd assortment of exercises in which you do a movement from your sport against added resistance. Examples: Sprinting up a hill, the football charging sled, putting a 20-pound shot (instead of 16 pounds), swinging a leaded bat, and pulling down a rebound against an elastic band.

You can make the resistance very strong, so that your movements are slow, or you can make it light, so that you can approach normal speed. But you must be careful to use this only as strength training. If you spend too much time moving around with weights holding you back, your form will suffer.

It is best to go through the movement in parts, if possible. For example, if you are trying to strengthen your tennis serve you could add a pound or two to your racket and try to go through the correct motion. That might develop more strength, but it would also ruin your serve. It would be better to move your racket through about one or two feet of the motion against the resistance of a friction-rope or an elastic band.

You can strengthen some of your running muscles in a variety of ways: wearing heavy boots or weights on ankles; running up steps or hills; running in sand, snow, or water; or running against the resistance of a rope or an elastic band.

One of the advantages of resistance work, besides specific strength training, is that you can use it to increase your muscle endurance. The more times you repeat it, the more it becomes an endurance exercise.

4. Weight Training

You can develop more strength, faster, with weight training.

If your sport requires medium or maximum general strength, you must do weight training. If any movement of your sport requires medium or maximum special strength, you can do it best with weight training.

If you have never done weight training, you will be better off if you can find a coach or athlete to teach you the correct exercises, methods, and safety precautions.

Most weight training is done with barbells or dumbbells. A few fortunate athletes can use a special weight machine. Or you can use wall pulleys, weighted containers (such as a sack), or a rope designed so that you can control its resistance by adjusting friction.

From a safety standpoint, if you are a beginner without benefit of weight coaching, you will be better off starting with the rope. You can buy one at a sporting goods store, or you can devise your own. (Wrap it around a smooth bar enough times to give you the resistance you want.)

Do not start out with the Olympic weight-lifting exercises. Those are special, competitive forms, which are more dangerous and less valuable than some other movements.

Your coach will give you some basic movements at the start, or you can consult a book on weight lifting in the library. In the meantime, here are some basic exercises often recommended for building all-around strength:

Clean and Press. Start with the barbell on the floor. Grasp the bar with your palms down. Your knees should be bent, your shoulders hunched, back arched, and arms straight down. Your first movement is a dead lift. Lift by pulling your shoulders back and pushing your hips forward until your back is straight. Next you "clean" the barbell: You lift it to a position in front of your chin with your forearms straight up. You next move is the "military press." Simply push the barbell up until your arms are straight overhead. You should add a toe lift for good measure.

Now lower the barbell in exactly the opposite manner and at the same speed.

This set of movements makes up the best all-around conditioner, adding strength to your legs, back, trunk, and arms. Start with a weight you can lift easily and repeat it several times, both as a warmup and to learn the proper movements.

The secret of weight training is "progressive overloading." That means you use enough weight to cause stress, but you build up gradually. The build-up, or progression, is done by adding weights to the barbell or dumbbells as you become stronger.

Usually, in training for strength, you do each movement 8 to 10 times. By the last movement you should be tired. When you progress to the stage at which you can do those 10 movements without fatigue, you should add some weight. The increases should be about 2½ pounds maximum, depending upon the movement and how much you are lifting. This is a matter of common sense; if you are lifting only 20 pounds in a certain movement, you would not add 10 pounds to it.

In the clean and press, if you work up to a weight somewhere near your body weight you will be strong enough to meet minimum general requirements. There is no reason to add more weight unless your sport calls for great strength. Also, there is such a thing as overdoing strength training. In most environments, when you have doubled your original strength you surely will have the minimum general strength required. After that you can either speed up your movements gradually, or you can increase the number of movements to 15 to 20, for added endurance. Or, of course, you can remain where you are by using only 10 repetitions at a time.

Abdominal Curl. This is a sit-up, but you bend your knees and arch your back to make your abdominal muscles work instead of the muscles that raise your legs. Hold your feet down with a barbell or piece of furniture.

You may need to start this exercise without weights. As strength increases, clasp your hands behind your neck. Then begin to add light weights, held behind your neck. Twist your body by touching your knees with opposite elbows.

Dumbbells. Use your creativity to invent arm movements holding onto dumbbells. Exercise every muscle in your arms and shoulders.

Bouncing Split Squat. If your sport includes running, this is a good general conditioner for leg strength. With a weight on your shoulders, leap up and land over one leg with the other extended to the rear. Do not pause, but immediately bounce up and reverse legs.

Other movements can be added for special strength. For example, shot-putters use the bench press, but it is of no value to most athletes. Decide which groups of muscles you must strengthen and how much strength they need.

You will benefit from some special strength work in any movement from your sport. You can strengthen your throwing arm by making the throwing movement against the resistance of the friction rope. The same can be done for your swinging movement, kicking, jumping, running, rowing, cycling, swimming, boxing—in fact, any movement imaginable.

When you go through actual motions, be careful to use a motion as close as possible to your correct form. In sports in which you swing something—such as baseball, golf, hockey, and tennis—attach the resistance close to your hands. This is necessary because the speed of a golf club, for instance, depends upon the free movement of your wrists. You develop power as far down as your wrists, but they must swing freely to gain a "crack-the-whip" effect. You could not move correctly with the resistance attached to the *end* of your club.

To retain flexiblity and the feeling of your correct form, you would be wise to follow each movement against resistance with the natural movement (without resistance).

You can lift weights every day if you have time, but when you become active with skill training you will not have that much free time. Once you have reached minimum levels, twice a week will hold that strength easily. If you need maximum strength, you will probably lose strength if you lift only twice a week.

One problem to watch while you are lifting weights is any change in weight in an undesirable part of your body. Experts claim that you can gain weight or lose weight as you wish while weight training. Shot-putters and football players want to gain weight. High jumpers and distance runners want to avoid extra weight. In most sports you do not want to add much weight, so here are a few tips:

- If you use light weights and many repetitions you will develop less bulk.
- If you develop only the muscles you need for your sport, no others will add to your bulk and those you use a lot will be held to a reasonable size.
- You can always reduce a muscle's growth by stopping your weight training of that muscle.

It is extremely important that you use safety measures when you train with weights. Severe injuries can result if you are careless. Several Olympic prospects have been lost because of accidents during weight training.

No matter what kind of equipment you use, you must lift correctly, with a straight back, and you must progress cautiously before increasing the resistance. That includes a warmup each day with lighter weights.

You can avoid much of the danger, especially if you are working alone, by using the friction rope or wall pulleys instead of heavy weights that can fall on you.

In using barbells or dumbbells, be absolutely certain the weights are fastened securely before you lift them. Be sure the floor and grips are not slippery. If you lift very heavy weights, have someone with you. Very strong men have been pinned down with a few hundred pounds across the throat.

5. **Circuit Training**

This is a series of exercises. Usually, you do each in turn until you get back to the first one. That is why it is called "circuit" training. The exercises are arranged so as to rest one part of your body while exercising another. In other words, you do not do all the leg exercises first and then change to arm exercises.

The primary purpose of circuit training is strength, but you can arrange it according to the requirements of your sport. It was originated so that several athletes could use the same equipment in an organized way, but you can profit from it and have a lot of fun even if you are alone.

The profit comes from making sure you do all the exercises and from the efficient way you alternate them so as to eliminate wasted time. The fun comes from competition against other athletes, or against time.

If you are striving for maximum strength—for football, shot-putting, or weight lifting—you will not emphasize speed in going through your training. But if minimum strength plus special strength in a few movements is your aim—as in most sports—you can go through the movements fast enough to give you endurance training at the same time. Endurance training is important in sports that require that particular kind of muscle endurance, notably basketball, hockey, boxing, soccer, tennis, handball, water polo, and the "racing" sports—running, swimming, cycling, and rowing.

Most of the exercises in your circuit should be against resistance, because this is strength training. But certain exercises that use your body weight as resistance—such as pull-ups, sit-ups, and push-ups on parallel bars—are suitable. In fact, if you are training alone, you should make up the whole circuit yourself. If you are a basketball player it will not do you much good to go through a circuit with a group of swimmers. You want your own exercises.

Once you have reached a satisfactory minimum level of strength, and if you do not need maximum strength, your circuit should be designed to maintain that minimum strength, develop any special strength you need, and promote flexibility and endurance.

That can be done in an interesting competition used by the Swedish modern pentathlon team. First, you test yourself in each exercise to find your maximum: how many times you can perform the movement before fatigue stops you.

In the competition, you do each of the exercises *half* as many times as your maximum. Time yourself and see how long it takes to go around the circuit three times. That maintains your strength and, at the same time, increases your anaerobic endurance and makes the whole thing interesting.

Anabolic steroids are taken by many athletes who need maximum strength. They do help increase strength, but they are not necessary for sports that do not require maximum strength, they are dangerous for teenagers and females (see Section E, Health), and they have possible bad side effects for male adults. Even fully matured shot-putters, weight lifters, football linemen, and wrestlers should weigh the risks before taking anabolic steroids.

You can do remarkable things with your body through weight training. The world record for the shot put is about 10 feet farther because of weight training. High jumpers average a gain of about six inches through weight training. Football players are incomparably better than twenty years ago because of this added strength and weight. Athletes in almost every sport improve through weight training.

Summary

1. Decide how much general strength you need for your sport—minimum, medium, or maximum.

2. Decide what special strength exercises you need for your sport.

3. Make a list of each group of exercises. Assemble them into one round of circuit training in the most efficient way you can.

(Separate similar movements from each other, but be practical about changing equipment.)

4. Collect the necessary equipment.

5. Start training at any easy level in each movement and progress only when your strength makes one level fairly easy.

6. Follow each strength test with a "shake-out" in which you stretch the muscles you just used. After special strength movements, go through the movement without resistance to maintain the correct "feel" for it.

7. Use weights that will hold you to 10 repetitions, and keep increasing weights until you have doubled your strength for minimum strength gains. (This is not to be taken as an exact figure. If you are already strong from doing some sort of resistance work, you need not double your starting strength.) If that is enough for your sport, use that level as your permanent training.

8. To go on to medium strength levels, continue to increase the weights as you master each one. This level should be about 50 percent higher than the minimum level.

9. To reach the maximum level of strength, either in general strength or in one or more special exercises, you must continue it indefinitely. That is seldom necessary, however, because maximum strength is rarely useful except in a very few special exercises such as the bench press for shot-putters. You have probably reached a level somewhere near maximum useful strength if you increase to four times your starting level.

10. Observe all safety rules.

11. Work on strength only one to three times a week during your competitive season, depending upon how much is needed for your sport.

C. SPEED AND QUICKNESS

Once there were two sophomore halfbacks on a good college football team. One was the star of the team; the other was second string. The second stringer went out for track and worked hard enough to become a contender for the Olympic team. In his senior year he was noticeably faster than the sophomore star, who was now second string. The track man went on for many good years as a pro football player, and the former star was never heard of again.

The moral of this story is that speed, which is necessary to so many sports, can be improved if you try, or it can deteriorate if you neglect it.

Running speed is a natural talent. If you are born slow, no amount of work will enable you to sprint faster than a man who is born fast. But work *will* enable you to sprint faster than you could before. In other words, you cannot improve your speed 300 percent the way you can improve your strength, but you can improve 10 percent and that can be worthwhile.

What is even more important, your start and pick-up can be improved the most. Almost anybody should be able to improve 20 percent in the first ten yards. Imagine how valuable those extra two yards can be in football, baseball, basketball, soccer, and tennis.

The most thorough way to acquire this speed is to go out for track. A year or so of sprint training will develop your natural speed to near-maximum levels.

If you are not fast enough to be a sprinter, or if your sport overlaps track season, or if you do not want to be a track man, the easiest way to improve your speed is still to work out with sprinters—if the track coach will allow it. If he will give you a few pointers and let you practice starts, you can learn faster than in any other way.

If you do not have the opportunity to be coached by a professional, you must work by yourself. If you understand the principles, and practice enough, you can teach yourself to be faster.

You can start understanding by dividing speed into three parts: start, pick-up, and maximum speed.

Start. A sprinter practices the start so many times that eventually he does not have to think about it. But the first time he tried it, the stimulus of the gunshot had to travel through something of a maze of nerve cells, with delays at all major connection points. He had to make a decision and send that message along other nerve cells to his muscles. Many muscles he did not need were activated, and he jumped and stumbled. His first move was much slower than when he touches a hot stove and a reflex action jerks his hand away. And his move was not efficient. Consequently, before he could start properly he had to learn a *fast* reflex and the *correct* reflex.

Nobody knows exactly how nerve pathways change so that response becomes a fast reflex action. You can study neuromuscular functioning and learn of several ways that speed can increase, but all you really need to know is that practice will make it possible to react immediately without thinking about it.

Many coaches have told their athletes, "Don't think." That sounds like some sort of joke, but it contains a lot of truth. Thinking takes time, so when a movement calls for quick reflex action, you must eliminate conscious brain work from the series of physiological actions between the stimulus and the response. When a sprinter hears the starting gun, it is as if he hears it with his legs, for they immediately explode into violent action.

Actually, his reaction is not immediate. Only a rare man, almost a freak, can react in less than one-tenth of a second. Since almost all athletes have reaction times within a range of ten to fifteen hundredths of a second, the speed of your reaction is not nearly as important as reacting *correctly*.

For a sprinter on the starting blocks, the correct reaction is to push with both feet. But in order to run, he must put one foot in front of the other, and so he starts with one foot farther behind the starting line, and that is the foot that takes the first step. He has taken a position that bends that leg at about 120 degrees, and so he gets the most efficient power. He is down low, almost parallel to the ground, because he wants all of his force to move him forward, not upward. (See how fast you can start if you stand upright with your weight on your heels.)

Some sprinters, especially those who are only beginning, can get off their blocks as fast as more experienced sprinters, but they fall behind almost immediately because they do not react *correctly*. For example, if their first step is only a short jab, it is a faster first step than experienced sprinters take but not as long. If they take a step that is too long, they lose time. The most efficient first step is about 1½ to 2 feet ahead of the other foot.

Once you have taken that first step as fast as possible, for the right length and in the right direction, you have started. Too many athletes make a false move. A basketball player, for example, often starts with the wrong foot. That means his reaction is wasted, for he stays in one place while his *front* foot moves. Then he must step with his rear foot (which should have made the first step), and that step is from farther away than it should be. That means it is too long, and too slow. His false movement at the start often means he is one step behind.

The start is also important in football, baseball, tennis, and soccer. The start is a skill, and you must practice it correctly until you learn it. A correct start toward first base can mean you are a full yard ahead, and that can mean the difference between "safe" and "out."

Pickup. You can gain another yard or more with a good pick-up, which is your acceleration between your start and the time you reach full speed. In most sports situations, you do not run far enough to reach full speed, and so your pick-up is that much more important.

The secret of a fast pick-up, in simple physics, is maximum power applied in the direction you are going.

Power comes from the force you exert with each foot in turn, multiplied by the speed of each stride. If you can use your strongest leg drive more often, you will go faster. If you can put more force into your fastest leg speed, you will go faster. If you can do both and still increase each stride a little, you will go faster.

You can increase your leg speed only slightly through practice. You can increase the force of each step greatly, through weight training. And you can increase your stride length by making proper use of your new strength through skill.

Probably the most important part of the skill you must learn is the proper body lean. Sprinters are taught this almost immediately, because of their crouch start, but many of them straighten up too soon and lose some of their potential power.

You must lean forward in order to keep your force behind you. If your force is directly under you, you will go straight up into the air. Therefore, when you are running at full speed your body should make an angle of 70 to 75 degrees with the ground. In the first stride or two of your start, your body should be at an angle of about 20 degrees. Thus, in your pick-up you change from a lean of 20 degrees to at least 70 degrees.

You can accelerate faster if you are leaning more. Your steps are shorter, which means that your foot remains in contact with the ground longer, which means that more force can be applied. Therefore, the shorter your steps the more you must apply this force *forward* instead of upward. Anytime you see a sprinter leap out of his blocks and straighten up in the first five yards, you know he is wasting too much of his power.

From this theory, it sounds as if you could run faster if you stayed at 20 degrees all the way. But you cannot lean that far, because as your strides become longer you would fall on your face.

Since each man is a different combination of leg speed and leg power, each man differs in his lean during pick-up. You can find your best angle and the distance you should hold it by experimenting. It is easy to know when you are leaning too much, but be certain you are not straightening too fast.

For the fastest possible pick-up:

- Lean forward so as to keep your force behind you.
- Use maximum leg power developed by weight training.
- Move your legs as fast as possible while increasing your stride with each step.
- Experiment to find your fastest combination of body lean and stride length. (Remember that you will increase your stride

and decrease your lean, gradually, until you reach full speed. That will require 30 to 50 yards.)

After you have developed your pick-up like a sprinter's, you can apply it to other sports. Football players and base runners already use a modified crouching start, but football linemen make contact almost immediately and so they must generate power with short steps. A base runner cannot use a full crouch because he must be prepared to whirl back to the safety of his base. In other sports—basketball, soccer, tennis, and handball—you must be upright to perform other functions.

The fact remains that you must lean forward if you want a fast pick-up. If you are a basketball player, on defense, and you suddenly see a stimulus—such as a loose ball or an interception—you want to move at the fastest possible speed. If you are on your toes, with your knees bent and your body crouched at an angle, you are in position to launch yourself into a fast start and a good pick-up. Even so, you must lean even more to get the maximum acceleration. If you are standing upright, on your heels with your legs straight, and if you try to reach full speed by running at your final, full-speed body angle—you will be *slow*.

Full Speed. Power equals force times velocity. In other words, your power is the product of how hard you can push away from the track and how fast you can make each push. But your power is not exactly equal to your speed. If you use your power inefficiently, you will not run as fast as you should. Your running form, then, is an important skill to learn.

The most obviously important part of your running form is the length of your stride. There is not much you can do about your leg speed, but you *can* find your best stride length and increase it slightly.

It is obvious that a longer stride means greater speed if leg speed remains the same. But runners differ in their use of this combination. Some take short and fast strides, while others take longer and slower strides. A good example can be found in the two great sprint rivals of the mid-1930's, Jesse Owens and Ralph Metcalfe. They were about equal in speed, but Owens had a stride of 7′3″ while Metcalfe's was 8′6″. Another runner of about their speed, Ray Norton, who was the world's best in 1959, had a stride of 9′3″.

As the strength of your leg drive increases, from strength training, your stride will increase naturally. You can also increase it by sacrificing leg speed, but that is not necessarily good. You must find your best combination of leg speed and stride length. That is the main part of learning correct running form.

It is obvious from the examples above that there is no best stride length for everybody. You must find the best combination for yourself. Probably the best way to do this is to start with a stride length that feels natural to you. Increase it with strength training, with high knee action, and with hip flexibility, and then experiment a little. You might try increasing it an inch at a time until your speed begins to slow. Then decrease it to about half way between your last natural stride and the slower stride.

High knee action is an important part of sprinting form. A high knee action helps you drive your feet down with more force, and it makes a longer stride possible. You need strength training to develop higher knee action.

The rest of your sprinting form is simply a matter of eliminating waste motion and effort. Your head and shoulders should ride along smoothly, without bobbing, wobbling, or swinging. Your arms should move straight forward from hip level to shoulder height and back again. Your arms balance your legs so that your hips do not roll. Your feet should make almost a straight line on the track, and you must not toe out.

You eliminate waste motion by relaxing every muscle you are not using. This is difficult for beginning sprinters because they think the more effort they spend the faster they will go. In a 100-yard dash, your best possible speed is while you are relaxed, but many sprinters struggle. In such a short race it does not hurt them seriously, but if they had to sprint over and over again, as in football, basketball, or soccer, they would tire too soon. You must learn to sprint without wasting energy.

Believe it or not, in sprinting the easier it feels the more effective it is. Tommie Smith was probably the fastest man who ever ran when he was at top speed, and he also looked smoother and more relaxed than most other sprinters.

Do not make the mistake of practicing sprinting at the beginning of your training period. You need four or five weeks of conditioning before you practice starts. You should have a few weeks of slower running, strength training, and much flexibility work before you try to sprint. Then you can work up to full-speed sprinting, but only with an easy running start. When you can handle that without injury, practice pick-ups without the start.

In other words, do it backwards. You should practice starts only after you are sure you are in shape for all the rest, because starts cause more injuries, and pick-ups the next most. Andy Stanfield was a great sprinter, but injuries threatened his career. By sacrificing his fast start and easing off the blocks he was able to run 220's, and he won the 1952 Olympic championship.

Once you work up to starting practice, you can do ten to twenty starts a day. At the same time, practice your pick-up to about 30 yards. This can be done about three days a week. If your sport is not track but still pays dividends for a fast pick-up, practice starting from a game position, but practice! You will probably have to do this before your regular training season begins, but you would be wise to practice pick-ups once in a while during your season. That extra yard or two is worth the effort.

You can learn quickness in the same way you learn to start fast. First, learn the exact technique, then learn to respond to the stimulus with that correct technique.

It is possible for you to have great reflexes, to be naturally quick in reacting to a situation, but to have the wrong reflex. A tennis teacher once demonstrated this to a student by unexpectedly tossing a ball at Don Budge. The famous grand-slam winner reacted unconsciously by taking his racket back. His reflex was in preparation to hit the ball. Most untrained people with fast reactions would move the racket toward the ball instead of taking it back.

If you begin by responding any way you can, you will probably learn some incorrect reflexes. Then you will have to "unlearn" them before you can master the correct reflex. Therefore, you can save much time and trouble if you learn the correct movement first.

Summary

Start faster by learning to react in the right direction.

Accelerate faster through strength and by keeping your weight out in front, ahead of your power. Improve your quickness of movement by learning technique, and then make it a reflex action.

D. ENDURANCE

Endurance is much more complicated than most people realize. Consider these examples:

A catcher smashes a long drive past the center fielder and tries to stretch it into an inside-the-park home run. He needs to run only 120 yards, but rounding third base he begins to tie up. He loses his lean, his leg speed slows, his stride becomes shorter, and he slows just enough to be thrown out. He lacks muscle endurance.

A substitute comes of the bench and begins to run up and down the basketball court. Trying to make an impression in the few minutes he expects to play, he hustles as hard as he can. He does so well the coach leaves him in, but after a few minutes he begins to tire badly. Then his man gets away from him and it costs his team a basket. He lacks anaerobic endurance.

A tennis player is in the fifth set of his second match of the day. He does not feel painfully tired, because he rests for a minute each time they change sides, and the points are short, but he notices he is beginning to miss routine shots. He tries hard, but his coordination is gone. He lacks glycogen reserves.

A cross-country skier watches his opponents slide away from him in the last five miles, but his legs will not respond. When he finishes he can hardly lift his legs. He feels weak and pale, and his hands tremble. He collapses and must be carried off. He lacks glycogen endurance and has low blood sugar.

An oarsman in a crew pulls hard to do his share of the work. His form is as good as the others' and he has as much endurance as they have, but in the last quarter-mile, when the cox calls for ten big ones, he cannot keep up. He catches a crab and they lose the race. He lacks the strength for proper endurance.

A great cross-country skier, with so much endurance he can race for seven hours, falls into a river while completely fresh. He knows how to swim, but after a few minutes he is so tired he drowns. He lacks endurance from capillary development.

A beginning track man runs as hard as he can several times a day trying to make the team. At first his progress is amazing, but after about a month he suddenly becomes slower. His blood has lost much of its oxygen-carrying capacity.

Endurance is a deciding factor in most sports. Lack of it causes a pitcher to be knocked out of the box after seven good innings. Fatigue causes a basketball player to miss the shot that would win the game. It can even cause you to miss an easy putt on the 18th green.

Your skill in any sport is controlled by your central nervous system, and your central nervous system must have carbohydrates for its metabolism. Thus, when you run low on carbohydrates your CNS does not function well and you begin to make errors.

A physiologist proved this by exercising a man until he was exhausted after an hour and a half. The physiologist gave him some glucose and the man was able to continue for another hour.

You immediately jump to the conclusion that you can avoid this simply by taking sugar in some form. It is true that long-distance competitors—runners, cyclists, skiers, swimmers, plus soccer players, tennis players, et cetera—sometimes take sugar during competition. But it is not that easy:

- Some people cannot stand sugar during exercise; it upsets their stomachs.
- You can absorb only about 50 grams of glucose from your stomach each hour, but you need 100 to 200 grams.
- In a few people, large glucose consumption triggers hypoglycemia, a condition much like exhaustion.
- Glycogen in your muscles is necessary for long periods of exercise, and it cannot be restored simply by drinking a glucose solution.

You can increase the glycogen storage capacity of your muscles by long and exhausting exercise. If your regular workout is about as long as your usual competition, you can force a greater glycogen storage capacity by exercising at least twice as long every two weeks.

That means hard exercise that makes you really tired. An easy walk will not do. A marathon runner, whose race takes around 2½ hours, sometimes runs for as long as 5 hours for this purpose. For any sport, jogging is the most efficient way to do it, unless your mode of transportation is swimming, cycling, skiing, or rowing.

There are two ways to *fill* your glycogen storage areas once you have enlarged them. One way is to eat carbohydrates during the day or two before competition. The other way is to rest from strenuous activity for at least two days.

An example of how these methods improve glycogen stores took place in a dramatic physiological experiment. Two men pumped one stationary bicycle, each using one foot, so that each man had one leg working and one resting. They kept at it until they were so exhausted they could not continue. Then biopsies were taken from the muscles of all four legs. These samples of flesh showed that the exercised legs had used up all of the glycogen, while the rested legs still had as much as when they started.

The men were fed carbohydrates for several days. After three days, their rested legs showed a slight increase in glycogen, but their exercised legs more than doubled.

This type of endurance can help you avoid loss of coordination near the end of long contests, like the tennis player who started ruining easy shots. But you should also take glucose at the rate of about 50 grams an hour. Your stomach may tolerate glucose best in liquid form. Many athletes take honey or fruit juices. Some add ordinary table sugar, but barley sugar is highly recommended. About 12 teaspoons equal 50 grams.

You cannot exercise for hours until you have built up to it gradually, as you built up your strength a little at a time. To understand aerobic training you must know a little about your body.

The muscle cells, which do the work of all your movements, are like little engines. They run on fuel and oxygen, like the engines in automobiles, but their fuel is carbohydrate instead of gasoline. You know about furnishing your muscles with fuel, but now you must consider your need for oxygen.

The word "aerobic" means "with oxygen," and so aerobic training is concerned with increasing the amount of oxygen to the muscles. Of the total increase in endurance gained from training, about 80 to 90 percent comes from increased ability to supply oxygen to the muscles.

You breathe in order to take in oxygen and to eliminate carbon dioxide. If you doubt the importance of oxygen, try exercising while holding your breath. The oxygen you breathe goes through your lungs into your blood, which carries it to your muscles. There it is used to burn fuel and give off the energy you need in order to move.

Your first problem is to get enough air into your lungs. Normally, you breathe harder when you need more oxygen, and so it is taken care of automatically. But when you are exercising hard enough to cause you to gasp for air, there is some evidence that you would have a little more endurance if you could breathe more oxygen.

Most people who want to take in more air expand their chests as much as possible, but that only adds air to the top of the lungs. The place where the oxygen is needed is at the bottom of the lungs, in the alveoli. That is where the blood lets off waste carbon dioxide, which mixes with fresh oxygen. That means that the air in the alveoli is only 14 percent oxygen, or less, while in the top of the lungs it is almost 21 percent oxygen.

If you can force out carbon dioxide, you will have more oxygen in the alveoli and your blood can pick up more oxygen. You can force out carbon dioxide by *exhaling*. No force is needed to inhale. All you have to do is expand the size of your chest cavity and air rushes into the vacuum. But to exhale as much air as possible you must decrease your chest cavity. This cannot be done with the chest muscles. It can only be done with a strange muscle called the *diaphragm*.

The diaphragm is a sheet of muscle shaped like a dome that separates the chest cavity from the abdominal cavity. When it flattens, that makes more room in the chest cavity and more air enters. You can force out much more air with the diaphragm than by making your chest smaller. Practice diaphragm breathing without moving your chest. Notice what you must do to force out the last possible ounce of air.

You should do diaphragm breathing whenever you have a "breather" during a game of basketball, football, soccer, hockey, tennis, handball, or water polo. Help yourself make room for more oxygen in your lungs. Diaphragm breathing can also help in continuous endurance sports, especially in swimming and rowing, where breathing is forced into rhythmical patterns.

Experts claim that careful breath control, especially exhaling, helps relaxation from tension. A pitcher often takes a deep breath before winding up for a pitch. That eliminates the need

for air during a movement requiring intense concentration on skill. You certainly would not expect a golfer to breathe while putting, nor would a basketball player breathe while trying a free throw. And yet if you are tired, you breathe faster. To slow down your breathing, you must eliminate as much carbon dioxide as possible by exhaling to the maximum one or more times.

If you take too many deep breaths you will become hyperventilated to the point of weakness and dizziness. Therefore, as you breathe deeply you should breathe more slowly. One woman trained herself to breathe so deeply that she breathes only four times each minute.

The second problem in aerobic training is to make the blood carry more oxygen. Almost 8 percent of body weight is blood, and about 55 percent of blood is plasma, which is 91 percent water. The other 45 percent of blood is made up of cells, mostly red cells. About 95 percent of the dry weight of red cells is hemoglobin. Most of the oxygen in the blood is carried in the hemoglobin. Therefore, the more blood you have and the higher the value of hemoglobin you have, the more oxygen your blood can carry.

The average person has about 4½ to 5½ million red blood cells per cubic millimeter of blood, and normal hemoglobin value is 14 to 16 grams per 100 cubic centimeters of blood. Athletes commonly increase their red blood cells to 6½ million and their hemoglobin to 18 or 19 grams, a tremendous increase in oxygen-carrying capacity. On the other hand, their blood cells and hemoglobin value can fall below normal because of destruction of cells.

In normal living, red blood cells are destroyed regularly. Average cells live only 120 days, and they lead a hazardous life. Each cell travels through the circulation in 45 seconds. It is squeezed in small capillaries and crunched when caught in a tightening muscle or when your weight comes down on it, as in walking or running. It must swell to take on oxygen and shrink when it releases oxygen. Eventually, it is simply battered to bits.

Severe exercise, if prolonged beyond 25 minutes, results in a

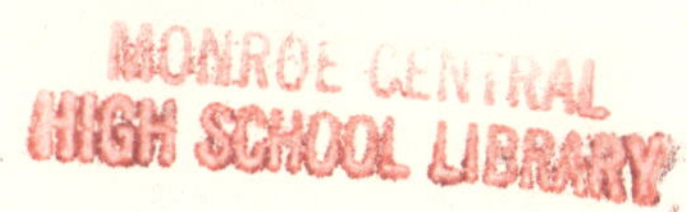

decrease in the red cell count and hemoglobin values. If you repeat this, day after day, your oxygen-carrying capacity can only go down. In addition to becoming a slower runner, you might regress to symptoms of weakness and discomfort: restlessness, irritability, aches and pains, loss of appetite and weight, pale skin, jaundice, dark stools, red urine, nausea, vomiting, diarrhea, abdominal pain, and shaking chills and fever.

All of this means that you must do what you can to increase your red blood cells and hemoglobin values and at the same time prevent as much destruction as possible. You can use four methods:

- Red cells are produced in your bone marrow when you have a shortage of oxygen, and so you will increase those values if you live at a high altitude. A man who lived at 17,500 feet all his life had a phenomenal hemoglobin value of 25.5. Lon Spurrier broke the world record for the half-mile with a surprise 1:47.5 after he had been at Mexico City's 7,300-foot altitude for two weeks.
- Training of the right kind increases your blood values. When you start to train, your red cell count drops because of destruction of cells and because your plasma increases and dilutes your blood. After a few months your values will catch up and you will have higher values than before—unless you train too hard.
- You need the right building materials to produce new red blood cells and hemoglobin. You need iron to build the heme of your hemoglobin, but iron is plentiful unless you live on refined foods. Most anemia is caused by a shortage of certain minerals and vitamins, particularly vitamins C and E. You can avoid this anemia by eating a well-balanced diet of fresh, unrefined foods, including liver. You can add insurance by taking vitamins C and E.
- You need rest before a major competition. Your blood values cannot be at their maximum unless you avoid severe exercise for a few days and give your blood a chance to increase

in value. Good runners have lost their superiority by donating a pint of blood. A distance runner went into a slump and showed so many symptoms that his blood was checked: His hemoglobin value was 14.8. He reduced his training, raised his hemoglobin more than two points, and ran well. Roger Bannister rested five full days before he became the first man to run a mile in less than four minutes.

The only way you can be certain of your blood values is to have a blood test, but your performance and other symptoms can give you a hint. Understand the physiology involved and follow the correct principles. Don't take a chance on failure at the time when you want to be at your best.

The third problem in aerobic training is to increase the amount of blood your heart can pump. The more blood pumped, the more oxygen reaches your muscles.

Your heart can increase its output in two ways: It can beat faster, or it can pump more blood with each stroke. When you exercise, your heart uses both methods to send more blood to your muscles.

Training will not increase your maximum heart rate. In fact, many well-trained distance runners show a slightly slower maximum pulse rate than nontrained men. All of your increase in output comes from developing a larger stroke volume. A well-trained heart can pump twice as much blood as the average heart.

You can increase the strength and stroke volume of your heart by exercise. The heart is a muscle. If you use it properly it will increase in size and strength and pump more blood. It follows the same responses to stress as your other muscles.

This stress should be applied gradually. Your heart does not strengthen if you sprint as hard as you can. It pumps at its maximum, which is too fast to be efficient. The result is that your stroke volume actually decreases.

The best level for training your heart is a stress that will barely force it to use its maximum stroke volume. If you go beyond this level of stress, two things happen: (1) your heart's stroke volume does not increase, and so you are wasting energy; and (2) you tire rapidly and stop exercising, and so your heart stops receiving any benefit. The best training for your stroke volume is a fairly mild level that you can maintain for as long as two hours a day.

Over a period of many years, your stroke volume will increase. That is why distance runners in former years were thought to be best at the age of twenty-seven or older; it took them that long to develop their hearts fully. But now, using better training methods, some runners apparently reach their top stroke volume by the age of twenty.

For an average young person, exercise that keeps your heart pumping at about 140 to 160 beats per minute is probably the best for developing a larger stroke volume. This is extremely important in the endurance sports and those that require much movement. Unfortunately, the sports themselves seldom keep your heart beating fast enough. If you count your pulse between points in a tennis match, for example, it is likely to be below 120.

The pulse rate is not an entirely reliable guide. Some people have naturally higher pulse rates than others. You should take your pulse sometime when you have worked very hard, to find your maximum. If it is 180 to 200 you are within a normal range and the 140-160 training range applies to you. But older people usually have a lower maximum pulse. If your maximum is 150, your training rate should be around 120.

It is also important how you count your pulse. It slows down rapidly when you stop exercising and can drop from 140 to 100 in less than a minute. It also slows when you sit down or lie down. Therefore, the most accurate way to judge your exercising pulse—outside of being wired electronically—is to count your pulse for only five seconds immediately after exercise and while still in the same upright position. Multiply by 12 and you have a fairly significant pulse rate for exercise.

Two hours of daily exercise at that level will give you a very strong heart, but you probably cannot stand that much work.

Many runners break up their total work load by training more than once a day. When Ron Clarke was the fastest distance runner he ran three times a day. For readers familiar with Dr. Cooper's "Aerobics" point system in which 30 points a week is recommended, note that Ron Clarke scored about 1,000 points a week!

Unless you are an endurance athlete, you will not want to work that hard, nor would it be worthwhile, because you would not have time or energy for your other skills. But you cannot develop your stroke volume satisfactorily unless you do *some* endurance work. Many tennis players run three miles or more each day, at an easy pace just below the borderline between aerobic and anaerobic training.

You can also obtain some improvement in your stroke volume with stop-and-go running, as in basketball or soccer. If you take your pulse a few times while you are stopped you can get an idea of your level of work. If it stays below 120 most of the time, you should supplement your training by running.

Some athletes, especially runners who compete at a mile or less, train with an "interval" method in which they run fairly fast for a short distance and rest by walking or jogging for about the same distance. This, too, will improve your stroke volume while giving you some speed training, but it cannot increase your stroke volume as fully as continuous running.

A fourth method of improving your aerobic capacity is through bringing the maximum blood to the muscles you are using. You can develop a large stroke volume by running, cycling, swimming, skiing, rowing, or chasing butterflies, but it does you no good unless the blood, with its oxygen, can reach the right muscles. The well-trained skier who drowned is a good example. He had the maximum stroke volume, but he could not force the blood into his swimming muscles because there were no pathways for the blood to take. These pathways are called capillaries.

When you begin to exercise, an amazing change takes place in your body. Blood stops flowing to places such as your stomach, which do not need it, and more blood goes to the muscles in action. This flow of blood through exercised muscles can be 50 times as great as when those muscles are at rest, because the tiny capillaries open and allow blood to flow through, one cell at a time.

The more you use a muscle, the more capillaries open along the muscle fibers. Physiologists have counted 1,050 open capillaries in one square millimeter of a dog's muscle. (A square inch contains more than 600 square millimeters.) You may find more capillaries than muscle fibers in a well-trained muscle.

Capillaries open where needed. Apparently, the blood forces its way between cells. After a tunnel is formed, it is lined with endothelium like that inside your heart and other cavities. This means that you develop capillaries simply by exercising a muscle; the more you exercise it, the more capillaries you open.

The *quality* of exercise has something to do with it. You will not open many capillaries if your exercise is too mild, or if your exercise is so severe that your muscles tighten and prevent blood from flowing. Any exercise that can be sustained for half an hour, but not four hours, is probably of the right intensity.

The most important principle to remember about forming new capillaries is that you must use a muscle over and over again for many hours. Some movements, such as pitching a baseball, are too violent to be repeated so often. You simply must make the movement at a slower speed so as to give capillarization a chance. You cannot have endurance in a muscle without a means of getting oxygen to it.

One other method of improving your aerobic capacity should be mentioned, although it applies to endurance as a whole. You simply cannot be an athlete without proper hormones.

Hormones help regulate most of the functions of the organs. You might think it is all automatic, but your hormones are extremely active when you exercise. They help regulate your breathing, the beating of your heart, the manufacture of new red blood cells, the level of sugar in your blood, the distribution of your blood, the working of your sweat glands, and many other complicated mechanisms of the most wonderful "machine" on earth—your body.

You need the hormone thyroxin from your thyroid gland to regulate energy output and the temperature of the cells. You need insulin from the pancreas to change sugar into glycogen, or fat. You need cortisone from the adrenal cortex during emergency stress. You need adrenaline from the adrenal glands to increase your heart's output, change glycogen back to glucose, and, in general, prepare your body for a maximum effort. Without your adrenal glands you would be dead in a week.

During the stress of sports and training, you need more than normal glands. Your adrenal cortex, for example, increases in size even more than a muscle when used. You can do three things to insure adequate hormone function:

- Have a thorough physical examination at least once a year, preferably after you have been under the stress of training for a while.
- Make your training program progressive. If you insist upon working as hard as you can, you are asking for trouble. You must avoid extremes. You can only adapt to stress by doing it gradually. And when you do stress yourself too much, balance it with the proper amount of rest; an easy day should follow a hard day.
- Furnish your body with the raw materials it needs for building hormones. Your body has the fantastic ability to maintain itself, but it cannot do it in a vacuum. It must have materials to work with. You never reach the stage of exhaustion before you have run out of raw materials.

The raw materials come from your food. You need a well-balanced diet with daily whole grain, liver, vegetables, protein, and supplements of vitamins, especially C, E, and pantothenic acid.

Pantothenic acid is one of the B vitamins. In a scientific experiment, men deprived of pantothenic acid became weak, tired, and ill, with high pulse rates, within 25 days. Pantothenic acid restored them to normal. Scientists have safely administered huge experimental doses as large as 15,000 milligrams of pantothenic acid daily. At the other extreme, the average American eats about 4½ mg daily. It has been estimated that an athlete needs 40 to 200 milligrams daily.

You can see, from all the mechanisms involved, that aerobic endurance is a complicated matter, and yet it is vital for athletic performance. Fortunately, the solution is relatively simple. In addition to breathing and eating properly, all you have to do is exercise steadily for many hours.

The exercise should be a movement used in your sport. For most sports, running is necessary, and thus running is the best conditioner; but swimmers must swim, cyclists must cycle, rowers row, and skiers ski. (Note: Cross-country skiers train by running when there is no snow.) If your sport is not a running sport, substitute your form of motion for running in the following plan.

You must develop capillaries before you can use your muscles enough to develop the rest. It is ridiculous to train your heart to pump a lot of blood before you have a place for that blood to go. Therefore, you must start out by running, even if you can run only a little at first.

If you are a beginner, start with jogging. Go as slow as you can for a few days. Do not let your heart pound along at 180 beats per minute. Do not let yourself get so out of breath that you cannot talk to someone as you jog.

Your progress depends upon your condition. At first your purpose is to increase the length of time you can jog. Your goal depends upon your sport. A distance runner should extend it to two hours, but others may stop at one hour. After you can jog a long time without discomfort, increase your pace gradually. Your maximum speed should be below the borderline of anaerobic running. That means you do not suffer the discomforts of producing lactic acid, and your pulse should not go over 150 for the average person. At the start of such a run, you should feel as if you could keep it up indefinitely. That feeling changes when your glycogen supply begins to run out, and so you should gradually slow down so as to be able to continue in relative comfort. Your last mile in an hour's run can be 20 seconds or so slower than your first.

The more time you put into this kind of running, the more aerobic endurance you will acquire; but most sports call for you to spend a lot of time on other skills, and so you may reduce this run to a half hour every morning.

Many athletes in running sports change to interval running after they have reached good aerobic condition, running at a faster pace for 110 to 440 yards and then jogging easily until they are already to run again. This helps more with speed and with anaerobic training, but it is not as good for aerobic training.

Another type of endurance you must build is anaerobic, which means "without oxygen." When you exercise so hard that your aerobic capacity cannot handle it, your emergency reserve of anaerobic energy can be used.

In each muscle cell a wonderfully complex series of chemical reactions changes glucose into pyruvic acid. When you can supply this cell with enough oxygen, the change continues aerobically and you have carbon dioxide, water, and *energy*.

You can use this energy to move muscles, but there is a definite limit to the amount of energy you can produce in this way. In addition, lactic acid accumulates and must be disposed of. The result is that even a highly trained runner cannot sustain a sprint for much more than 30 seconds. After that he begins to slow down toward a pace that can be supported by his aerobic capacity alone, and with his glycogen gone his coordination suffers and he ties up, struggling as if he were running under water.

To improve your anaerobic endurance, you must use this mechanism many times. It is a chemical reaction, with definite limits, and you can improve it only a little, but that little is extremely valuable. It is the difference between being safe and out on an inside-the-park homer. It is the difference, in that last minute of the basketball game when you are dead tired, between beating your man down the floor or seeing him get away to win the game.

Everyone has some anaerobic endurance to start with. Young people have quite a lot. A 13-year-old girl can run a 440 at a fairly good clip. This natural anaerobic endurance can be improved in several ways:

- Aerobic training helps. Glucose changes to pyruvic acid in the same way before the decision is made, and so aerobic training develops part of the mechanism you need. It has been estimated that you reach about 90 percent of your anaerobic capacity simply through complete aerobic training.
- Each time you go beyond your aerobic capacity and produce some lactic acid, you are training your anaerobic mechanism; that means any time you sprint 50 yards or so, as in wind sprints, or with much shorter runs in basketball, tennis, football, and handball. Unless you rest for a minute or so between bursts, your lactic acid level will increase. You might play one of those games for an hour or more with a constant level of lactic acid. That is excellent anaerobic training. The endurance sports, of course, call for your maximum lactic acid level in competition.
- You can do specific anaerobic training. No one knows exactly the best way to reach maximum anaerobic capacity, so it may be best to play it safe and run up your maximum lactic acid level several times to "stretch" your capacity to its maximum. This should be done no more than twice a week for perhaps a month before your competitive season begins. If you intend to compete in one of the endurance sports—running, swimming, cycling, cross-country skiing, or rowing—you will probably reach your maximum more often than that.

You can overdo anaerobic training. Heed all the warnings about too much stress leading to failing adaptation. If you go all-out too often—such as several times a day—you will sooner or later fail. You will lose your blood values and your hormone protection and be worse off than if you had done no special anaerobic training at all.

It may seem strange to have to issue warnings not to overdo something that is very unpleasant and even painful. But athletes, especially young ones, are so eager to succeed that they will try anything, and some of them think the harder they punish themselves the more endurance they will have. That is not true. Year-round aerobic training, plus the anaerobics of your sport, plus one month of special effort will give you the maximum anaerobic capacity.

Two other improvements can add to your endurance: strength and form. Strength has already been discussed. It adds to endurance simply by making each movement use less energy. For example, if your leg can press only 200 pounds it has to work much harder to move your body than if it can press 300 pounds, and the harder work is tiring.

Form will be discussed in the next section, under skills. Good form includes relaxation of all muscles not being used for a particular movement. Any muscle that is not relaxed is using energy, and in many cases a tense *opposing* muscle forces you to use much more energy than you should in the proper muscles. Thus, good relaxed form is an important aid to endurance.

Summary

1. Everyone should do some aerobic training. Start with jogging. (Substitute other movements, such as swimming, if your sport calls for something other than running.) After you can jog indefinitely, increase your speed to develop greater aerobic capacity, but do not go into anaerobic running.

2. Twice a month or so, run a long distance—two hours or more if possible—to increase your glycogen reserves.

3. Give your blood and glands a chance by providing your body with the proper raw materials. Eat a well-balanced diet—see the next section—and add vitamins C and E plus pantothenic acid.

4. Do some special anaerobic training just before your competitive season. You may benefit from two all-out sessions a week for about a month for running sports. You need more for the endurance sports and less for sports such as golf, table tennis, and high jumping.

5. Be sure your strength is adequate for your sport.

6. Learn correct form, and relax all muscles you do not need.

E. HEALTH

The subject of this section may surprise you, but consider this: What if you do all the training possible and make yourself the greatest athlete in the world, and then, the day before your most important competition, you injure yourself or become ill?

An injury or illness can defeat the greatest talent and perfect training.

You are like a car in the Indianapolis 500. You may be the fastest one there, but if you can't finish the race you are worse off than all the slower cars that do finish.

In addition to missing important competition, illness or injuries can cause you to miss important training.

If you learn to maintain good health, that knowledge may be worth more to you than everything else you get from sports.

You cannot learn the whole subject in a brief discussion, but you can start thinking and you can seek more information. The subject of health can be divided into three parts: hygiene, injuries, and nutrition.

1. Hygiene

Medical examination. Before you begin training, and periodically thereafter, you should be examined by a doctor. You cannot injure a healthy heart unless you are sick, but be sure your heart *is* healthy. You should also rule out any other obstacles, from anemia to poor eyesight.

Cleanliness. It is surprising how many people are careless about personal cleanliness. Millions of deaths could have been prevented simply by keeping clean. This includes bathing, washing after contact with anything on which foreign bacteria may live, cleaning your fingernails, brushing your teeth and hair, and avoiding anything that might enter your body and make you ill.

Isolation. Three feet of air space between you and a person who is spreading germs is the best rule for avoiding infection. Avoid, if possible, anyone who is sneezing, coughing, or snuffling. Kissing is especially dangerous; your chances of missing a season with mononucleosis are excellent if you kiss a lot of people who are kissing a lot of other people.

Avoiding stress. Your training is stress, and you have a limited supply of adaptation energy. A combination of fatigue from training, improper clothing, and some bacteria can halt the greatest athlete. Cold, hot, or wet weather are stresses, and you should protect yourself against them. A baseball pitcher who wears a protective jacket while he is not pitching is not a sissy.

Eating. The rule about keeping unknown foreign material out of your mouth applies to food as well. If the food or the place where it is prepared does not look sanitary, don't eat it. And don't drink water indiscriminately; know its source and know it's fresh.

Smoking. One of the stupidest things any human can do to himself is to form the smoking habit. It will shorten your life, reduce your heart's function, decrease the oxygen-carrying capacity of your blood, prevent some oxygen from leaving your alveoli, constrict your small blood vessels, and halt the action of cilia whose job it is to clear your lungs of dust.

Alcohol. Small quantities of alcohol affect coordination. Liver damage, quite common from alcohol, limits the liver's ability to convert protein to carbohydrate and lactic acid to glycogen. Even a little beer affects the body's heat regulatory mechanism and curtails the release of oxygen from hemoglobin. Alcohol kills brain cells by the thousands, and nobody can replace brain cells.

Drugs. Most athletes are too interested in taking care of their minds and bodies to risk destruction from drugs. Even the weakest of stimulants—coffee, tea, cocoa, and cola—can produce insomnia, irregularities of the heart, and stomach trouble. And even the weakest hallucinogen—marijuana—combines the dangers of smoking, including cancer-producing carcinogens, with loss of coordination. Continued use almost surely means that you will drop out of athletics and anything else that requires self-discipline. In large doses, marijuana can have the same effect as strong hallucinogens, including delusions, panic, depression, and psychosis.

Some athletes are tempted to use drugs in an effort to improve their performance, even though that is cheating and can bring suspension from some sports for life. Some are tempted to take a depressant to relieve anxiety and let them relax. These pills also cause confusion, loss of coordination, weakness, and a tendency toward accidents, none of which are of much help in sports. Other athletes may be tempted to take pep pills, but, in addition to many other bad results, amphetamine has been proved to cause a significant loss of efficiency.

One of the leading physicians in sports medicine, Dr. Ernest Jokl, states flatly, "Not a single instance is known in which an athletic record has resulted from the administration of drugs."

Anabolic steroids, used to increase weight and strength, are derived from male hormones, and so you are playing with fire if you take them. They are definitely out for females. In teenage boys, they may cause bones to mature too early and thus stunt growth. The most commonly expected side effect is an ultimate reduction in the size and power of the testicles, something not many men would trade for a slight athletic advantage. The American Medical Association has issued severe warnings about possible harmful effects.

At best, anabolic steroids should be used only by fully mature males who want to take a risk in order to develop maximum strength.

Sleep. Your need for sleep is an individual matter. The only certainty is that you need more sleep if you exercise hard.

Olympic coach James Counsilman reported the sleeping habits of two of his great swimmers. Bill Utley slept 10 hours when not training and 12 hours when training. Chet Jastremski slept 6 hours normally and 7 hours when training hard.

Lack of sleep delays recovery from workouts, which makes the next workout unsatisfactory. If you cannot get enough sleep at night, supplement it with a nap, preferably after your afternoon workout.

Colds. You will not catch cold unless you are exposed to someone who has a cold. People have lived through extremely cold weather and chills without colds. But if you cannot escape exposure, defend yourself as well as possible by avoiding other stress, by eating an exceptionally well-balanced diet, by drinking lots of water, and, some people say, by taking vitamin C.

If you do catch cold, you can still train at an easy level, putting emphasis on skills, not on strength or endurance. With a fever or sore throat, you need complete rest. Some doctors are faster to give medication than others, and you should know that prescribed drugs usually have side effects that delay the return to full training ability.

Athlete's foot. You can prevent this infection by drying thoroughly between your toes. If you shower where many others also bathe, wooden sandals will help protect you. Most school showers have footbaths for your protection.

2. **Care and Prevention of Injuries**

Most teams have a trainer to treat injuries, but it is much more fun to prevent them.

One of your best weapons against injury is common sense. Don't go out for crew and row for an hour the first day unless you want blisters. Don't ignore a new pain that persists for an entire workout. Don't rush into new activities of a violent nature. It is only common sense to protect yourself.

Injuries come from one of two sources: from sudden, violent action or from gradual wear and tear.

You can protect yourself from the violent kind by avoiding foolish chances and by using proper safety equipment.

The most important part of preventing wear-and-tear injuries is to locate the cause. A blister, for example, is never the result of a single movement. If you feel a hot spot during movements, locate the cause and eliminate the friction or you will develop a blister. If you are spartan and continue, after a few days you will have a callus. After a few weeks you may have a corn. If you cannot remove the cause, then you must protect the area.

When you start to warm up, sometimes you feel aches and pains. Actually, if you are aware, you have some sort of ache or pain almost all the time, even when you are inactive. You must learn to recognize the difference between discomfort, soreness, and injury.

Discomfort and soreness normally disappear as you warm up. An injury will usually feel worse. Therefore, if the pain gradually disappears, continue training, but if it becomes worse, you must stop that action. It is not spartan to train on an injury; it is foolish.

If you have a real injury you can often do some other kind of training. A foot or leg injury, for example, will still allow you to swim. You can develop endurance while swimming, and the water will help your injury heal faster. A basketball player with an injured leg might shoot free throws or do strength training. Don't waste any more time than you must.

Muscle injuries are the most common of all injuries. If you suffer a violent injury, the sooner you can put ice on it, the better. (Cold water or a chemical cold kit will also help.) When you first touch ice, it feels hot; then it feels cold. After two or three minutes it should begin to ache. Then, after eight or ten minutes, the ache disappears and the area becomes numb. You should keep the ice on the injury for a few minutes after it feels numb.

Ice treatment is a first-aid measure. If a trainer is available, he will take over. If not, and if the injury seems serious, see a doctor.

After two or three days, a muscle injury is usually treated with heat. General heat, such as a hot bath, is not as good as specific heat, because the purpose is to stimulate activity at the location of the injury.

The best kind of heat is moist heat, but it is difficult to maintain for hours. The best way is to use a waterproof heating pad over a wet cloth.

As an example, a tennis player pulled a small muscle attaching to his spine. He tried rest for a week at a time, but the injury persisted for seven months, through diathermy, sound-wave treatments, cortisone shots, and heating pads. Then he learned about moist heat. He soaked a small towel in hot water and wrung it out. He spread the towel over the injured area, put the heating pad over it, and held them in place with a wide elastic bandage criss-crossed over his shoulders and around his chest.

He plugged the heating pad into the nearest electric outlet and kept moist heat on his injury while he ate, read, watched TV, and slept. He kept it heating for as much as twelve hours a day. He continued to play tennis, but the seven-months-old injury healed within a month. Moist heat is close to miraculous.

Here is what to do for some specific injuries:

Blisters. Avoid friction, especially in new shoes. One handball player always had blisters on his toes while he broke in each new pair of shoes. Finally he began to wear shoes a half size larger, and he had no more trouble with blisters. (He added an extra pair of socks to take up the slack.)

Be aware of hot friction spots in new shoes or other equipment. Rub friction spots with Vaseline. If you must train or compete anyway, tape the area and wax the tape.

Small blisters may disappear before your next workout. If not, puncture with a sterile needle, and tape the area.

Bruises from continuous pounding can be prevented with protection, or by removing the cause. Heel bruises are most common. You can protect your heels with plastic heel cups.

Sprains. Some sprains can be avoided by running only on safe surfaces. Rink Babka, one of the world's greatest discus throwers, lost an almost certain place on the 1964 Olympic team because he sprained an ankle while running in the dark.

If you cannot avoid rough surfaces, tape your feet and ankles to prevent sprains. Another way is to take even a bad fall rather than try to take your weight on the side of your foot.

A sprain will heal itself with rest, but you do not want to rest that long. Ice treatment, followed in two or three days by moist heat and gradually increasing exercise, will cure it fastest.

Do not, except in the most extreme emergency, submit to taping and a painkiller for a sprain. Without pain to act as a "psychological splint," you can do far more serious damage. This principle applies to other types of injuries as well.

Arch problems. Most arch trouble results from strains and can be handled like a slight sprain. UCLA trainer Larry Carter has an exercise to strengthen arch muscles: Stand on a towel and pull it under you by moving your toes.

A fallen metatarsal arch can be relieved by taping a pad under the arch before each workout.

Shin splints. This pain in the shins comes to runners, basketball players, tennis players, and others who run for training. The cause is not fully understood, but it is easier to prevent than cure.

To prevent shin splints, avoid pounding, especially when you begin running. Stay off hard surfaces at first, wear cushioned shoes, strengthen and tape your arches, and use correct running form—light and with no toe-out. An exercise to help prevent shin splints is called the Tucker Twist: Sit and force your foot in all directions with both hands.

In treating shin splints, you must first remove the cause. Rest plus moist heat and massage will heal the condition.

Tendon soreness. Achilles tendon soreness forced out such great runners as Ron Delany, Al Lawrence, and Don Bowden. It results from overstretching or overworking. It can happen if your heel sinks too low, as in running on soft ground, or uphill, or in spiked shoes after training in flats or barefoot.

Successful preventive measures have been arch supports (tape your foot or your shoe), a built-up heel, and stretching exercises such as the Tucker Twist.

Stitch. The cause of this sharp pain in the side or abdomen varies, and it is not fully understood. It happens mostly to people who are not in good condition and near the beginning of a workout.

Arthur Lydiard, the great running coach from New Zealand, says stitch is causes by tight muscles in the chest and stomach throwing pressure on the diaphragm and straining its ligaments. He advises strengthening and flexibility exercises such as bending, plus much running.

Pulled muscles. Anyone who sprints has a chance to pull a muscle. If you work into condition gradually, and if you always warm up thoroughly, both by stretching and by running, you will lessen your chances of a muscle pull.

If you do pull a muscle, wrap it in a compression bandage, apply ice, and treat it like any other muscle injury, limiting activity to a level that produces no pain.

Cramps. Usually a cramp occurs instead of a pulled muscle. In stop-and-go games such as basketball, tennis, or soccer, your leg may cramp while you are stopped or barely moving.

Cramps are caused by fatigue, lack of salt, heat or cold, or dietary deficiencies. They can usually be prevented by taking salt tablets before competition, but since excess salt is bad for you, experiment in training without it.

Chafing. Vaseline will help prevent chafing.

Heat exhaustion. This is a shock reaction to exercise in hot weather. You can prevent it by proper acclimatization, drinking liquids during long competition or training, and taking salt.

Common sense will prevent many injuries and help in healing the rest.

3. **Nutrition**

The average diet in the United States, richest nation in history, is not adequate for athletes.

The good food is available, but most people do not eat it. Instead, they satisfy their cravings with junk foods. An athlete needs raw materials to build useful blood, to replenish hormones for adaptation energy, to rebuild muscle tissue, and to increase glycogen reserves. All your energy, and your very life, comes from the food you eat.

Most people cannot tell you the constituents of a balanced diet, and even more people eat food they know is not best for them. Athletes need better food than nonathletes, because of their greater requirements for energy and building materials. Thousands of scientific tests confirm this lack, and yet little is done about it. You can only learn for yourself and apply what you learn.

First, you must always be aware of nutrition and strive for a well-balanced diet. An athlete may burn as many as 6,000 calories a day, but they should be properly balanced between fats, proteins, and carbohydrates. Extremely active athletes need up to a gram each of protein and fat per pound of body weight and up to five grams of carbohydrate.

In percentages, that is 15 percent each of proteins and fats and 70 percent carbohydrates. According to experts, if most people had a choice from a large variety of foods they would choose 15 percent proteins, 45 percent fats, and 40 percent carbohydrates. If so, your conscious change is to switch about 30 percent of your calories from fats to carbohydrates.

But each of the three must be balanced. The carbohydrates should be about one-third sugars and two-thirds starches. Fruit and honey are included in the sugars. Starch comes from cereals and vegetables.

The proteins must balance to give you all of the amino acids. The most complete proteins are found in eggs, milk, liver, and kidneys. Other good protein sources are meat, food yeast, nuts, soybeans, and cereal germ.

The fats should balance toward the unsaturated, which means that they are relatively free of hydrogen. Liquid fats—vegetable oils and fish oils—are best. Saturated fatty acids are found in solids such as margarine and meat.

To balance the diet also means to avoid extremes. You should eat a variety, including fiber, liquids, vitamins, and minerals.

In some parts of the world, people live on only one food group, but it is best to eat some of each. The major groups are: meat (including fish and eggs), vegetables (including fruit), milk (including butter, cheese, and yogurt), and cereals (including bread and rice).

Possibly the best general plan is to eat a variety of foods that include those four groups, but to avoid certain foods. If you avoid junk food that fills your stomach, you will put into it only good foods.

On that theory, you cannot go far wrong if you avoid fried foods, refined foods, greasy and spicy foods, and sugary desserts. That would cut out of your regular diet such popular foods as hamburgers and milkshakes, hydrogenated peanut butter and jelly, potato chips and soft drinks, hotcakes and syrup, chili beans, most dry cereals, and most desserts.

If most of your food is fresh, balanced, and not from the "avoid" list, your diet should be satisfactory. And yet athletes may still be short of certain raw materials. Scientists are continually discovering new shortages. Here are a few supplements you should consider:

- Vitamin C. You can obtain 100 to 200 mg of vitamin C per day from foods, if you plan for it, and that should be enough for normal living. But the adrenal glands use vitamin C to synthesize the hormones you need. It is used in the release of glycogen from the liver and the repair of muscles and tendons, and Russian sports scientists consider it a necessary stress vitamin. They recommend a supplement of 330 mg a day. Indiana's great swimmers use it. It has other nonathletic values, it is cheap, and it cannot harm you. Vitamin C is lost in sweat, an important fact in athletics.

• Vegetables and fruit. For some reason, vegetables are neglected in the American diet, even though they are a fresh food one step closer to the source of energy—the sun. Much evidence shows that vegetables help clean poisons from the liver and blood. The Russian scientists claim that the alkalinity of vegetables increases endurance, and they recommend that 15 to 20 percent of calories should be from fresh fruits and vegetables.

It is interesting to note that when foreign athletic teams visit the United States and are offered a large variety of foods, their most popular choice is not expensive steaks or highly refined foods, but fresh fruit. Also, many fruits are so delicious that first-class restaurants offer them for dessert.

• Vitamin E. In addition to its value in building blood and hormone strength, vitamin E is effective in building stronger hearts, and tests prove that it increases the use the body can make of oxygen. Racehorses have been improved by using vitamin E, and rats that were deprived of it showed degenerative changes in muscles and endurance.

Scientific estimates of the average person's need for alpha tocopherol (the important kind of vitamin E) range between 20 and 170 mg daily. The diet suggested by the U.S. Research Council contains only 6 mg, and much of that is lost. On that basis, everyone would be wise to supplement diets with vitamin E, and athletes certainly need more than other people.

• Pantothenic acid. Like vitamin E, pantothenic acid is in short supply in the U.S., where the average daily intake is only 4½ milligrams compared with the 40 to 200 mg recommended. The more stress you are under, the more pantothenic acid you need.

• Salt. Salt is obtained from vegetables, and food is usually prepared with some salt. Many experts recommend no salt in addition to the above, except for an extra teaspoon during the first few days of hot-weather exercise.

Lack of salt can lead to cramps, muscle tremors, and a feeling of weakness similar to that resulting from low blood sugar.

• Liquids. A minimum of two quarts of liquid daily is needed for survival. That includes the water in food. In addition to that amount, you must replace all you lose during exercise.

Experts calculate that if you lose 2 percent of your body weight by sweating, your efficiency is lowered. Some distance runners have lost 7 percent. (Two percent of a 150-pound athlete is 3 pounds, equal to 3 pints of water.) Drinking fluids during prolonged exercise will definitely improve performance. Gone are the old superstitions about avoiding water during the game. Marathon runners must have it; why should basketball players avoid it?

You can determine your water loss easily by weighing before and after exercise. Calculate it at one pound per pint of water. Experts have calculated that you can remove no more than 1.8 pounds of water from your stomach each hour, so it will do you no good to drink more than that amount.

It is important not to enter a long, hot competition already partially dehydrated. The great New Zealand coach Arthur Lydiard advises his runners to drink all they want on the day of a race. He once entered a race with milk and liquids "sloshing around inside" him and set a record.

• Other vitamins and minerals. Most people do not eat properly, so they can benefit from taking one of the capsules containing most of the vitamins and minerals. They do it as "insurance," to play safe.

One of the important aspects of food is what you eat before a competition. You should begin thinking about it two days beforehand. Cut out rough, greasy, spicy foods. Eat bland carbohydrates, easy to digest.

Your last meal should be about three hours before competition, although fruit juices are beneficial if taken only an hour before. Protein and fat should be cut out of this pre-event meal. There is no need for caffeine or other stimulants; you will be excited enough.

If your sport calls for prolonged severe exercise, you need extra fuel. A liquid meal is easily digested and can be of benefit during competition. But even glucose needs half an hour to be useful.

Experiment with different kinds of feeding during training, especially juices. Then know which foods agree with you during exercise.

F. TRAINING EFFICIENCY

You want to increase your strength, your speed, your endurance, and one or more skills. You know how to increase the first three, and we shall soon discuss skills. But how will you find time to work toward all these different goals?

You need a lot of time, or you must use what time you have efficiently. If you have a lot of time, it does you no good unless you use it. Most successful athletes train all year, and many of the best train twice a day.

But if you are like the majority of people, your time is limited, so you must learn to make the best use of your available time. Here are some time-saving methods to consider:

Make wise use of your time. Each time you learn a skill correctly, you save much time in the future. It may cost you a few extra hours at first to learn the proper form, but once you learn it, you save a lot of time.

Each time you learn a faulty skill, you lose much time in the future. You may save a few hours at the beginning, but the longer you put it off the harder it will be and the longer it will take to learn correct form.

Save time on other activities. Be an efficiency expert. Work at saving time on various activities. Here are a few suggestions:

• Sleep. There is evidence that people do not need as much sleep as they get. You may be able to reduce your night's sleep by one or two hours if you do it gradually. A nap of fifteen minutes may be worth as much as a whole hour tacked onto the end of a night's sleep. Experiment, but do not deprive yourself of rest you need.

• Work. If you work by the hour, you cannot reduce that time. But if your work is school homework, you can fit bits of it into small segments of time. For example, if you must spend an hour working mathematical problems, you need not wait until you have a whole hour free. You can work for two minutes between periods, fifteen minutes while waiting for supper, half an hour during your lunch period, five minutes while waiting for the bus or a friend, and a few minutes after practice. Most people "waste" an hour or more every day between activities.

• Chores. Every day you have some little jobs that take up some of your time. You can spend half an hour after practice in the shower, dressing, combing your hair—or you can do it in half the time. Those extra minutes are valuable; save them, and use them.

Find opportunities to train. Your efforts as an efficiency expert should extend to your training time. Make it count. If you try, you can do more training in less time. Here are some methods:

• Establish priorities. Some parts of training are more important than others. For example, suppose you are a basketball forward doing some shooting practice during the off season. If you shoot from wherever you recover the ball, you will do a variety of shooting, but it will be haphazard. But if your greatest need is to develop your shot from the corner, make that your first priority and practice it most of the time. In an hour you might take 60 to 100 shots from the corner, but if you left it to chance you might take only ten.

• Do it faster. Some training can be done faster than it is usually done. For example, shooting baskets from the corner means wasting a lot of time chasing the ball. If you use three balls, you save some time. If you can invent a ball return by building a slope that will roll it back to you, you will save even more time. Or a helper might do the same job.

You can save time by organizing your training the way a coach does. Know everything you want to do so that you lose no time moving from one activity to another. Anybody can be efficient if he tries.

• Divide training into pieces and fit them in. You don't need a full hour to shoot baskets; you can shoot for ten minutes at a time on six different occasions. Find an unused bit of time and put it to use.

Jim Ryun did this by lifting weights during the few minutes between runs. He had to rest his heart and legs before he could run again, but that did not stop him from doing weight training.

• Combine two activities. Sometimes you can find a way to do two things at once. Endurance training, for example, can be combined with most activities. If you keep moving so fast that you build up lactic acid, your anaerobic endurance is being trained. If you keep moving enough for your heart to beat 130 to 160 times a minutes, you are doing aerobic training. If you plan such training to last an hour, you can eliminate your aerobic run for the day.

Strength training, in the form of resistance training, can be either anaerobic or aerobic, depending upon how much rest you allow yourself between movements. And, of course, it is speed training when the resistance is light and you do it fast, such as two men pushing the charging sled in football.

In games where an opponent might counter your movement—as in basketball, football, tennis, hockey, handball, boxing, wrestling, and water polo—it is to your advantage to be able to make the right movement as fast as possible. Once you have perfected a skill at normal speed, practice making the same movement faster. This is a combination of skill and speed. An example, from tennis: Once you learn how to turn your body and take the racket back, practice doing it faster by standing closer to your opponent.

Probably the best combinations for saving time are two skills —any two movements that go together will do. In boxing, for example, if you are drilling yourself to slip a punch, you can at the same time practice a punch of your own.

You will need a little effort and ingenuity, but if you are willing to try you can save a lot of time.

CHAPTER • III

How to Perfect New Skills

A. HOW TO LEARN TECHNIQUE

Do you remember how you learned to ride a bicycle?

Actually, you may remember learning to ride—how impossible it seemed at first and how easy it became later on—but you may not know *how*.

Even scientists do not understand all the complicated details of how the neuromuscular system learns to remember all the complex movements of a new skill. So you are not expected to know the details, and you have no need to know. But you will become a better learner if you understand some of the general principles, and it is a fascinating subject.

Few things in this world are as interesting and yet as unappreciated as the kinesthesia, coordination, memory, and reflexes that combine to make up neuromuscular skills. Consider each of them:

• Kinesthesia is the sense of the position of the body. You can check on this in a simple way. Close your eyes and think about your hands. Without looking at them, you know the exact position of each finger. You can tell how much each is bent and where it is pointing. If you lift your hand, you can feel where it is and what movements it is making. Without looking, touch the tips of your fingers together. You can also sense the position of your head, legs, and trunk, and when you move you know what is moving and where.

• Coordination is something else you take for granted. You think it is easy to reach out, pick up a pencil, and write your name, yet you are using many muscles to accomplish that small task. Without coordination you could not do it. If you used too much strength, your hand might fly up and hit your face. If you did not use enough, you could not lift the pencil. When you write, you must move the pencil in the right direction for exactly the right distance. Each movement requires a different set of muscles. Each set of muscles has an opposing set that can make exactly the opposite movement, so when you make one movement, the opposing muscles must relax. Most movements require a remarkably complex coordination between several muscles and nerves, contracting each muscle exactly the right amount while relaxing all the others.

• Memory. If you had to think of each muscle and nerve as you used it, you could make only the simplest movements, and those would take a long time. Fortunately, you have a memory. Exactly as you remember where you live and how to get there, you remember how to move the pencil to write words. No scientist is exactly certain how you do it, but you can store millions of memories. You cannot perform all the coordinations necessary to ride a bicycle the first time you try it, because you have no memory of the necessary kinesthesia, coordination, and reflexes. After all those complicated requirements are in your memory, you can ride a bicycle with ease.

• Reflexes. Think about riding a bicycle. When you begin to fall off balance a slight fraction of an inch, you are warned by your senses—your eyes, the balancing mechanism in your ears, and your kinesthetic feelings. You have in your memory the necessary coordination of nerves and muscles to correct your position. But you do not have time to think of all those things. You are thinking about something else. And yet you respond with the correct coordination to the stimulus of being off balance—*without thinking.* That response, which bypasses your conscious mind, is called a reflex. (More properly, it is called a "conditioned reflex" to distinguish it from your *un*learned reflexes, such as blinking when something threatens your eyes.)

As stated above, no one knows exactly how all these remarkable feats are accomplished by your body. But somewhere in your brain and spinal cord, the area of your central nervous system, these feats of control and coordination take place with a speed and exactness that put a computer to shame. In fact, the most remarkable control feats accomplished by a computer are merely copies of this human achievement, done in a limited way according to a prepared program that originated in a human brain.

In order to learn a skill, you must use these powers in the right way.

The first step is to lump all of these powers into one system, since they interact with each other. Because it is not part of your conscious mind, think of this system as a mechanical tool to control your skills. Call it your Control System.

Your Control System works like magic, for you are not conscious of anything happening and you do not know how it happens, and yet wonderful results take place.

For example, if you ever tried to learn a dance step, you probably had difficulty at first. Your feet seemed heavy, clumsy, and stupid. You thought it would take several more sessions to learn the right sequence of steps. You waited several days, without practicing the step, and then tried it again. You were agreeably surprised at how easy it was the second time.

Something obviously happened inside you. Somehow, you now had a memory of how to coordinate, and a rudimentary reflex enabled you to do it as fast as the music demanded. You were not perfect, but you were definitely better and on your way to mastery of one more skill. How did it happen?

No one knows how it happened. If a pathologist performed an autopsy on you, he would not find anything different than before. It all took place along the pathways of your nerve cells, in such mysterious places as your brain, your memory, your central nervous system—your Control System.

No one knows the exact physiological changes that take place when you learn a skill, but people *do* know how to make those changes take place. When you learn to use your Control System, you will have the secret of learning and *improving* all sorts of skills, athletic and otherwise.

To begin to understand how to use your Control System, consider a hypothetical example. Suppose you were alone on a beach and you found a frisbee—something you had never seen before. In the absence of any written instructions, you would have no idea what to do with this plastic plate. You might wear it like a beret, or use it to scoop sand or water. Being of an active nature, you *might* try to throw it, but your effort might be to see how high it would go, or how far it would roll, or how much of a curve it would make.

But if you were with an equally ignorant friend, you might accidentally start to throw the frisbee back and forth between you. Then you might begin to compete to see who could throw it the straightest. Gradually, if you kept at it for an hour, you would begin to throw it straighter and straighter.

How? Simply by discarding methods that sent the frisbee plunging to the sand or twisting off to one side, and using methods that made it sail straight. In other words, by trial and error.

But how do you know which methods are right and which are wrong? Your arm, wrist, and fingers move in a complicated way, and your conscious brain cannot keep track of all those movements. The answer lies in your Control System: It knows right movements from wrong.

How does it know? After all, you could spend an hour doing all sorts of things with a frisbee and not learn any skill. The difference now becomes obvious, and you have learned the first and most important means of controlling your Control System:

You must give it a goal.

Without direction—without a goal, a purpose, an objective—your Control System will not work. Until you *want* to throw the frisbee straight, you might do anything with it. Even when it sails straight by accident you will not react with any pleasure, because you do not care whether it goes straight or curves.

When you give your Control System a goal, it may try many different methods, but it always discards the unsuccessful ones and keeps the others. When you learned to ride a bicycle, your Control System began to eliminate all of your movements that caused you to lose balance. Now you can sit on a moving bicycle and make the delicate balancing movements without giving them a thought. In fact, you probably do not know, in your *conscious* mind, how to do it. But your Control System knows, and it will not forget easily.

Learning most athletic skills is harder than learning to ride a bicycle because they are more complicated, but the principle is the same. Give your Control System a goal and it will help you reach it, within your physical limits. You cannot ask to drive a golf ball 600 yards and succeed. Perhaps your absolute physical limit is 350 yards. You might then learn to drive 300 yards on occasion.

Why the difference? Why won't your Control System enable you to drive 350 yards? The answer is complex. To reach your absolute limit you must develop your strength and flexibility to the maximum you can use. You must have exactly the right club and ball. You must have the best possible fairway and weather. And, most of all, you must have only the best possible swing.

Doesn't your Control System give you the best possible swing? Not unless you tell it exactly what you want.

That sounds confusing. It sounds as if your Control System cannot make you better than your physical limits allow, and it is limited in another way: It works by trial and error, like a guided missile, correcting itself whenever it goes off course. Thus, if you only tell it what you *want*, it will select the first method that seems to give some sort of success. If you leave it alone it will continue developing this faulty method, and more practice will only increase your ability to perform it. After a while it will become very difficult for you to change, because your Control System learns *well.*

You can see examples of this on almost any golf course. Look at that sixty-year-old man who hits a wide slice on every drive. He has perfected it through so many years to the point at which he knows where to aim his drive so as to slice into the middle of the fairway.

Perhaps in the same foursome is a younger man who is trying to learn to drive straight down the fairway. He hits a slice that goes out of bounds to his right. On his next drive, he over-corrects and hooks into the rough on his left. Once in a while he hits a drive straight down the middle. He is not as good as the older man because he is wild, but if he keeps trying he will be better eventually because he is still directing his Control System toward a better swing. But if he is like most golfers, he will not practice enough to give his Control System enough choices, and he will never reach perfection. In other words, each man compromises at a certain level of imperfection. One chooses to groove an imperfect swing, while the other chooses to progress by nearly blind trial and error.

It does not have to be either way. You can choose a better way. Instead of relying entirely upon your Control System like the older man, or mostly upon your conscious mind like the younger man, your conscious mind can take charge and guide your Control System.

You can do this by giving your Control System a clear picture of what you want it to do.

It is not enough to say you want to swing hard and have the golf ball land in the fairway 200 yards away. You must picture in your mind the flight of the ball. It is not enough to say you want to swing your driver any natural way that gets results. To avoid learning methods that will restrict you in the future, you must picture a correct swing.

That is best for you because of the way your Control System operates. It uses trial and error, true, but if you consciously accept a faulty swing, your Control System has no way of knowing that the swing was faulty. Therefore, it records it as satisfactory and enters it in your memory. Thus you are more apt to repeat that swing in the future.

Your Control System "remembers" only your successful swings. The more of one kind of swing you have in your memory, the easier it is for you to make that swing. That is why the sixty-year-old slicer is so consistent: He accepted his slice and perfected it. Now, if by accident he hit a drive with less slice, his Control System would record it as unsatisfactory, and it would not enter his memory.

But if you give your Control System a clear picture of a good movement, nothing else will pass inspection by the kinesthetic-coordination part of your Control System.

Your job, then, is to choose the best possible goal (considering your limitations) and send the clearest possible picture of it to your Control System.

There are six methods you can use to accomplish those two aims. All of them help you communicate a clear picture to your Control System, and all except the last one help you select the best form. Use them in the following order:

• *A Coach.* Your first choice should be a competent teacher. A really good coach has the knowledge and experience to give you everything you can get elsewhere plus two other important items: (1) he can handle you psychologically and inspire you to great efforts; and (2) he can observe you in action and help your Control System correct your errors.

You can inspire yourself if you really want to succeed, and you can use moving pictures of yourself as an aid, but you cannot reproduce the overall knowledge and experience of a good coach. You will be wise to seek one out when you begin.

On the other hand, the last three methods can be used only by you. A coach can suggest them and guide you in their use, but you must operate them yourself. Therefore, the ideal way to communicate with your Control System is to start with a competent coach and use your own powers in addition.

After you learn your skills, a good coach can help you perfect them, correct faults, and groove the best possible form. Then he can help you put them all together and use them properly. In team sports, and in a complicated sport like tennis, proper *use of skills* is sometimes more important than perfect execution.

A coach, therefore, has many values, and he can often help you more than you can help yourself. But you should not follow a coach blindly. You should study your sport and become an expert as soon as possible. Then you will be able to judge your coach. If you are sure he is inexperienced and wrong about a certain point, try to discuss it calmly and maturely at the proper moment. If he is mature and not too busy, he will cooperate with you. If you are right, perhaps you can persuade him. Many of the best coaches freely admit that they have learned from their athletes.

Keep in mind that this procedure is for learning an individual skill, not a choice of team play. In individual sports when you hire a professional to teach you—as in golf, tennis, bowling, boxing, and skiing—you have every right to select a man you believe is competent. But in team sports, and especially in high school, you must accept reality and make the best of it.

Some high school coaches are highly competent, dedicated men who deserve your full confidence. Others, however, are teachers assigned to coach on the side, and sometimes they have neither the training nor the desire to be good coaches. If you must accept such a coach, do all you can to feed your Control System the proper information.

The next five methods can be used with or without the guidance of a coach.

• *Observe.* The quickest and easiest way to send clear pictures of good form to your Control System is to watch good athletes in action. You can watch the actual competition or you can see it on television. You can also gain much from a series of stationary pictures that can be flipped to give the illusion of movement. These have the advantage of being available for "instant replay" one picture at a time.

Whichever you use, do it before you go very far into your learning program. Self-taught athletes often spend most of their practice time trying to correct habits they would not have if they had started by seeing it done correctly.

What about all those athletes you watch who have faults in their form? To work best, this method demands that you see good form. If you watch several good athletes, most of what you see will be good form and your marvelous Control System will reject poor form.

Of course, you should use judgment about which athletes you observe. You must become a critic of form, and this is the place to begin. If you can watch a national champion and analyze his strengths and weaknesses, you will have no difficulty feeding information to your own Control System.

Your most important habit, if you want to benefit from observing athletes in action, is to watch their *form*. You might watch a tennis match for two hours the way most people watch and have only a vague impression of form. But if, instead of watching the ball all the time, you watch how a player gets his racket into position to make his stroke, the memory pool of your Control System will be greatly enriched.

Most tennis spectators do not know how a player gets to the net after his serve because they watch the ball while he is moving in. Casual spectators seldom see the receiver's footwork and racket handling, because they are watching the ball travel the length of the court. They come away with an excellent picture of a ball, but no picture at all of some of the important parts of the game.

For that reason, force yourself to watch the important details of individual action instead of the broad sweep of the game. If you are a football linebacker, watch the linebackers; don't try to follow the ball through the line. The ordinary football spectator collects many fine pictures of how to be a quarterback, but what if you want to be a center?

When you first begin to observe, before you have had time to become an expert on form, you must use judgment about which athletes you watch. Obviously, you should watch golfers on the pro tour instead of hackers at your local club. In every case, unless you have other information, you may assume that the better athletes have the best form.

Another way of making an early judgment is to assume that the more graceful athlete has good form. Some of the best movements in athletics look *easy*. That is because perfect coordination requires you to relax all other muscles, so the movement flows smoothly, using only the essentials. Also, the perfect movement comes from your Control System without any hesitation or indecision. When a movement is partially controlled by your conscious thought, tension can enter at any point and cause an abrupt or jerky movement. For these reasons, if you watch the graceful athlete you are more apt to be watching the best form.

A word of warning: Many good athletes have peculiarities of style. Do not let yourself be confused by *style* in contrast to form. Style is often a movement of a part that has nothing to do with the important athletic movement. For example, Emil Zatopek, winner of four Olympic gold medals and holder of every world record at distances longer than three miles, had a terrible style. His head wobbled, his tongue flopped out, his shoulders hunched, and his arms sometimes reached straight down. But if you watched his leg action you saw no wasted movements at all. And after all, he ran with his legs. Don't let yourself be distracted by unimportant gestures, like a magician directing your eyes away from his crucial movement. Watch the essential movements.

To gain the most from observation of good athletes, you must study. Watch first, to get a general idea of what it is all about. Then study before and after each observation. The next two methods are a discussion of study.

• *Read.* A great many books and magazine articles have been written about form in various sports. Many are not thorough enough, but most will give you a general idea of the most important points to consider.

The written word can give you certain advantages over someone who merely watches athletes. It can tell you *why* a certain movement is best done in a certain way. It can explain why a short man swings a golf club one way, whereas a tall man must use a more upright swing.

A detailed analysis of correct form may mean very little to you —or your Control System—unless you read it carefully enough to visualize it. You must "see" it as vividly as if you watched it, or did it yourself, in order to impress it upon your Control System.

Written instruction can do two things: (1) analyze the movement in detail; and (2) give you an impression of how the movement should feel. If you read several descriptions of correct form you should be able to put together in your mind, and in your Control System, a detailed description based on a consensus. Even if one or two descriptions contain errors and others leave out important details, you can learn the correct form if you read enough.

But you cannot learn solely by reading about it. Your reading must be in conjunction with these other methods, especially the next one.

• THINK. Although your Control System is outside your conscious thought, everything that enters it must go through your conscious mind. Your Control System is the servant of your conscious mind. Your mind gives the orders, and your Control System tries to carry them out. It does the actual work. You certainly do not want your Control System working under an incompetent leader. Consequently, you should *think*.

It is possible to be a good athlete without being an expert on form, but those are the athletes who reach a pinnacle of success while everything is going right and then suddenly disappear from the scene because they do not know how to hold their form. Many a big-league batter hits well for one season, or part of a season, then never does it again. But when a natural hitter also thinks enough to become an expert, he turns out to be Ted Williams. There is no guarantee that you will ever be good, even for part of a season, if you do not learn correct form.

Your thinking begins when you ask yourself *why*. You can

grasp the *how* of it rapidly, from a coach, a book, or by observing; but when you figure out why it is done that way, you are beginning to think.

For example, in learning to swim the crawl you are told to apply power over the full length of your arm stroke. You see good swimmers reach far forward to start a stroke, and you see them end the stroke behind their hips, and so you use a straight arm pull. It seems logical, because you are applying force against more water than you can with any other arm position. But after your Control System learns this method you see some underwater pictures or drawings and are told the fastest crawl stroke uses a bent arm.

If you are on your own, or your coach is too busy to think for you, this will not make much of an impression, and you will probably continue swimming with a straight arm pull. But you will use the correct form if you understand *why*.

When you understand that the initial force of your straight arm pull tries to lift your body straight up out of the water and the final force pulls your body down, you will change to a stroke designed to use all possible force to pull your body in the direction you want to go.

To understand the *why* of correct form, you must think about what causes movements and motion. In other words, you must learn some elementary physics. It might be helpful—but it is not necessary—to learn Newton's three laws of motion and the meaning of such terms as force, power, inertia, law of conservation of momentum, and others. More important, you should use common sense in analyzing cause and effect.

Of course, this depends upon the extent of your common sense. You learn common sense by observing what happens under certain circumstances and by drawing conclusions. You might draw the same conclusion from studying physics but fail to make a common-sense application of the principle.

As an example, suppose you are a football lineman. Your goal is to block an opponent. You realize the importance of moving faster than he does, and so you spring off both feet and hurl your body at him. You do beat him to the punch, but your effort fizzles out and he leaves you on the ground. You learn to apply continuous acceleration by repeated application of power toward the ground, which reacts as force toward your opponent. Or you can use common sense, which tells you that once you leave the ground you cannot change direction or add any power to your drive.

Sometimes, common sense even triumphs over science. At one time certain scientists went to great lengths to prove—on paper—that a pitcher could not throw a curve ball. At the same time, anyone with common sense could simply watch the ball curve.

Since common sense is sometimes slow and sometimes absent, however, it is best to use any source of truth you can. If your coach or your book tells you why, check it with your common sense and then accept it. If no ready answer is available, try to figure it out for yourself. You'll be surprised what some concentrated thought can do.

If you know why one way is right and another is wrong, you will learn faster, you will learn more correctly, you will be able to hold your form more consistently, and you will be able to correct your mistakes more surely.

Knowing *why* is sometimes very simple and sometimes complicated. For an example of a simple law of physics, take the long jump. All you are trying to do is jump as far as you can. It is obvious that the faster you run before your jump, the more momentum you will have and the farther you will jump. With that in mind, most beginners try to increase the force of their speed with their last step. But it stands to reason that if you could apply extra force to your forward speed you would do it on every step and run that much faster.

Actually, your effort at the takeoff must be for *height*. The higher you go, the farther you will travel at the same speed. Thus you should think solely about height after you have reached top speed.

An example of more complicated physics is the golf swing. It is simple enough to know that the ball will go in the direction your club is moving when it hits the ball, *if* the face of your club is perpendicular to that same line of flight. And the speed of the clubhead determines the speed of the ball. That is simple force and simple direction.

But the head of your driver is making two curves when you hit a drive, one vertical and one horizontal. If either of those curves does not straighten out in time, it will impart torque, or spin, to the ball. On the horizontal curve, this will cause a hook or slice; on the vertical, a topped drive or one that zooms up at the end and falls short. In any case, according to the law of conservation of momentum, if there is spin on the ball, part of the force of your drive is wasted in rotary motion.

Whatever your sport, some physics is involved. If you really think about it you can figure out what you need to know. Here are a few laws to keep in mind:

—Once any kind of object is launched through the air, its center of gravity continues in the same direction unless another force is applied to it. (A ball thrown in outer space would go straight indefinitely.)

—The center of gravity of any object has as much weight on one side of it as on the other, in any direction. (Your center of gravity is probably in your abdomen.)

—The most common force that changes the direction of an airborne object is the force of gravity, and the heavier the object, the more force. (You cannot put a 16-pound shot as far as you can throw a baseball.)

—The next most common is the force of wind. (You must always be aware of the effect of wind on any moving object.)

—If a ball is spinning fast enough it will curve in the direction the front of the ball is moving. (Odd-shaped objects are exceptions. A discus, for example, must have a gyroscopic spin like a frisbee to maintain its steady flight through the air. The spin of a football around the axis of its direction also steadies its flight.)

—All of the force applied to a ball is used. If none of the force is dissipated in spin, the ball's initial speed will be equal to the force. (The more spin you put on a ball, the slower it goes in comparison to the force you exert.)

—When a moving ball strikes a flat surface, it rebounds at the same angle to the opposite side of a right angle. (Example: In a tennis half-volley, if you hold your racket perpendicular to the court, the ball will be rising when it strikes your strings and it will continue to rise at exactly the same angle when it leaves your strings.)

—The distance any object travels is the result of both force and velocity. (The power of a glacier can move a mountain, but it cannot knock a Ping-Pong ball half an inch. A paddle weighing only a few ounces cannot budge a mountain but it can drive a Ping-Pong ball at a speed of 50 miles per hour. Thus, to move your body or a 16-pound shot, you need both speed of movement and strength of movement.)

—Force, in athletics, is the result of energy. (Examples: The energy you apply to a golf ball with the speed of your clubhead plus the compression of the ball; the energy you put into your fiberglass vaulting pole by the speed of your run; the energy you put into the string of your bow by pulling it back; the energy of your football block equals your speed plus his; the energy you put into your swimming stroke is reduced by the resistance of the water against your whole body; your energy in distance running must be conserved by using a minimum of lift.)

—Centrifugal force is greater if you use a longer lever. (Examples: A round-house hook, delivered with a bent elbow, will not travel as fast as your extended arm in a discus throw. And your extended arm cannot travel as fast as the head of your golf club. Thus, in baseball, the longer your bat, the less you choke it, and the nearer the end you meet the ball, the faster the ball will go.)

Think about every part of each movement in your sport. Start with what you are trying to accomplish and determine the best physics to get the job done.

If you think enough, you can become an expert. That gives you many advantages. Some were mentioned above, but one of the most important is that you are not exactly like any other athlete, so correct form for you is slightly different from others'. If you are an expert, you can make those slight changes.

Once in a lifetime an expert can even improve upon the accepted form in an event. An example was Parry O'Brien, who invented a new form for the shot put and added many feet to the world record. Another was Dick Fosbury, who revolutionized the high jump. Over the years, expert players and coaches have changed the accepted form in most sports. Perhaps you can do the same.

One added fringe benefit is that if you become an expert in your sport you will be in demand as a coach or teacher.

These four methods of communicating with your Control System—a coach, observation, reading, and thinking—are the obvious ones, but two others take place inside you.

• *Feel.* This method is really the reverse of the others. In all the other methods you show correct form to your Control System; in effect, you say, "Here is how I want it done. Copy this method for me." To use this method you work in the opposite direction. You wait until your Control System presents you with an example of good form and say, "There! That's how it should be done all the time."

You cannot depend upon this method, because it happens rarely and almost by accident. But when it does happen you should use it.

You use it simply by calling attention to it. If possible, stop all further activity for a while and think about it. Remember exactly how it felt. Go over it in your mind a few times. You might even stop your workout or change to another activity so as not to superimpose a faulty form on your memory.

When you make a perfect movement you will recognize it. Not only will you be successful in your movement, but every part of it will feel "right." All your kinesthetic sensors will approve; nothing will feel wrong. You will have no feeling whatever of having forced yourself through the movement with conscious control. It will feel so easy you will be surprised.

When you are fortunate enought to make such a "perfect" movement, you have the best possible model to show your Control System, and that is the best possible way to communicate with your unconscious System. Make as much use of it as you can, especially with the last method.

• *Imagine.* Many people might think you are wasting your time in idle dreams if you imagine yourself making the correct movements of perfect form, but you can actually improve your technique by using your imagination. In controlled experiments, people have improved significantly in such skills as dart-throwing and shooting free throws with no other practice than in their imagination.

It sounds like black magic, but it has a simple explanation. The neuromuscular system, in fact your entire Control System, does not know whether the picture it receives is real or imaginary, and it reacts in the same way in either case.

For cxamplc, supposc you arc walking alonc at night. Suddenly, among the dark shadows, you see a darker shadow in the shape of a man lurking in wait for you. Your heart leaps into a pounding beat. Adrenaline pours into your blood, preparing you for flight or fight. Your muscles tense, ready for action. You may even run, or at least shy away from the danger. And yet you do not now whether there is real danger or imaginary danger. You do not know whether a man is lurking there, or only a shadow. Your unconscious mechanism reacts in exactly the same way in either case.

The inability to know the difference can harm you or help you. If you send negative, defeatist thoughts to your Control System, it will react to the picture you present to it. Almost anyone who has ever played golf has had the experience of hitting several drives in a row either straight or with a slice until you come to a hole with an out-of-bounds on your left. You think, "I must be careful not to hook here," and you step up and hit your first hook of the day.

The white magic of imagination can work wonders, too. A former softball player learned that a game was scheduled for a gathering he was to attend several weeks in the future. He had been an excellent hitter who hit very few home runs, but in the fifteen years he had been away from the game he had often thought he should have tried to be a power hitter. He knew that a full swing with correct timing—waiting for the ball—would have added many home runs to his total.

He began to imagine hitting a home run in that future softball game. Over and over again, he "saw" the ball coming in straight over the plate a little above his waist, right where he liked it. He "felt" himself waiting until the ball was over the plate before his bat met it. He "felt" the clean contact of bat against ball and "watched" it soar high beyond the center fielder's head. This was not the same swing he had used during his playing days, but now he wanted to hit a home run.

The day of the game came, and he went to bat without any batting practice. The first pitch missed the plate, but the second ball came straight over the plate, a little higher than his waist. He waited, exactly as he had imagined. He took a full swing, straight and long. He stood watching, almost forgetting to run, as the ball soared high beyond the center fielder's head. It was his first time at bat in more than fifteen years.

Another middle-aged man stood in the YMCA gymnasium during the intermission of a folk dance. Some of the men were swinging on the rings. He had never done any gymnastic work and, in fact, had always been a little afraid of such things. But suddenly he imagined himself running toward the rings to get up speed, grasping them with both hands, flying into the air with a complete somersault, and landing on his feet.

And he did exactly that.

Ben Hogan, whose skill with a golf iron has seldom been matched in any sport, performed each shot in his imagination before hitting the ball. He "felt" the perfect swing and the clean hit before trying it. That was his way of telling his Control System what to do.

Of course, before you can imagine the perfect form you must

have some idea of what it is. You must gather information—from your teacher, from reading, from observing, from thinking, and from feeling—and from your own picture of what you want to do. Then you simply "see" and "feel" yourself doing it, and you "see" the perfect result. Your Control System can then come closer to perfection.

Now that you know the methods of teaching your Control System to do what you want it to do, you need to know how to organize and conduct your efforts. This is called "practice."

B. PRACTICE

You must practice to learn your skill, to perfect it, and to retain it. Then you must practice *using* it correctly.

Practice is a tool that will give you a great advantage in almost any sport because the large majority of athletes, including the professionals, do not practice enough or practice in the wrong way.

Practice—of the right kind—is the surest way to get ahead.

One reason your opponents do not practice as much as they should is that they dislike it. Of course, if you are playing only for fun and do not care whether or not you learn any of the skills, you need not practice.

But the type of person who *wants* to succeed can feel great pleasure from learning. Each bit of progress in learning a skill is a small triumph in itself, to say nothing of the hundreds of times you will use it in the future.

Each athlete seems to have his limit, at which repeated drill on a skill becomes drudgery instead of fun. One athlete can practice for four hours, while another is impatient with fifteen minutes of drill. To solve this problem for yourself, you should consider two points: efficiency and your need.

Efficiency of learning requires at least daily practice while you are learning a skill. But once your Control System has learned all it can about performing that skill, you can retain it with occasional practice. Some experts have concluded that 20 to 30 minutes of practice is best for one skill. Once you have perfected that skill, you can retain it by using it in competition or with only a few minutes of practice each week.

Your need for drill should determine how much time you spend on it. While you are learning the skill, you need short but frequent periods of effort. Then you must drill until you perfect it. That may take anywhere from a few hours to thousands. Your practice time, then, will depend upon your hurry. If you need a thousand hours and you practice one hour a day, it will take you three years. At three hours a day you can reach the same perfection in one year. If, like many mediocre golfers, you never practice, you will remain mediocre.

Thus, your desire to succeed is the main thing you need to make practice acceptable. Still, the more pleasant you can make your learning experience, the more you will learn, so there are other ways to make practice more enjoyable.

One, which is really part of the above, is concentration. If you concentrate on learning, your mind will enjoy it; if you merely go through the motions of a drill, you will be bored and uncomfortable.

Most people are happier with other people than when alone, so you will tolerate practice better if you do it with someone else or even where others can watch you.

Your surroundings make a difference. Many distance runners dislike the boredom of running around and around the same track, so they run across the countryside, watching the scenery and people as they go. If your sport permits, choose varied and pleasant surroundings for your practice.

Make practice competitive and keep score. That not only improves your concentration, but it increases your interest and sometimes makes it fun. If you are a basketball player practicing free throws, a hundred practice shots could be boring. But it is interesting if you are trying to break your record for the most successful shots out of 10, out of 20—out of 100, for the most in succession, for the most without touching the rim, et cetera.

Do not overdo your drill. After you are warmed up, if you seem to be performing up to your maximum ability there is certainly no need to keep drilling until fatigue or boredom causes you to slip. After all, you do have other skills to practice, or other ways to practice this one skill.

You have three stages of learning. The first stage is learning the technique, as discussed in the previous chapter. The second stage is perfecting that skill, which means drill. The third stage is learning to *use* that skill properly. To illustrate the three stages, consider how to train for one of the most demanding sports of all from the standpoint of skill—tennis.

At first, you must learn *how* to make each stroke: forehand, backhand, service, volley, half-volley, lob, overhead, drop shot, slice, chop, and other variations; then you must drill to perfect them. This requires thousands of hours. But then you must also learn to *use* your strokes correctly. Each of your strokes is used in a different way against speed than against medium pace or a slow ball. Each differs depending upon how high your opponent's ball bounces, and each differs according to where you want to hit the ball and how hard. This is extremely complicated, and most tennis players never learn the whole combination of shots.

The same thing might be said of a football quarterback. First he must learn to throw a pass accurately. Then he must learn to hit a moving target at various distances. Then he must learn to do it while several huge men are trying to knock him down. There is not much point in trying to learn the fundamentals of throwing an accurate pass in a game while dodging tacklers. The fundamentals must be learned first. And yet there is not much point in hours of drill at a stationary target after you have learned to hit it.

You must progress from one stage to the next and upgrade your practice accordingly.

Even the first stage—learning the technique of each skill—sometimes requires gradual progression. A controversy still exists among teachers as to which is the best way to teach a skill:

by the "whole" or by "parts." One reason people cannot agree on which method is best is because each skill differs.

For example, it is impossible to break down the parts of a complicated dive and practice each separately. When you dive, you do the whole act each time. But a tennis stroke, which is a complicated movement, can be broken down into parts with great benefit to the learner.

You could practice the backhand drive for years and never have a good one unless you learn to turn your body to the side and beyond. So, with a beginner who has no bad habits from playing while facing the net, why not start by learning to turn the body into position? Then he can learn the correct swing. After he has learned to turn and swing correctly, he can begin to learn to time the ball exactly.

You can see that some skills are learned more easily if you break them down into parts instead of trying the whole movement at once. Unfortunately, this is seldom done, and people go through an entire career with faulty form that could have been avoided with two or three hours' work at the beginning.

On the other hand, you do not want to spend too much time working on one part because it might become more difficult to coordinate it with the whole. For that reason, another method—called "progressive parts"—is favored.

In the progressive parts method you learn one part of the skill and then add a part to it, practicing both together.

Of course, whether you start with the whole movement or reach it in parts, once you start using it you always correct and improve each part as you can.

The most important principle to keep in mind when choosing which learning method to use is this: Do not keep any faulty part.

That means you must go back to fundamentals and learn correctly whenever a fault becomes a habit, whether it is in the first hour of learning or in the thousandth hour.

A general rule, then: The more complex the skill, the more you use the progressive parts method instead of starting with the whole movement, unless, of course, you cannot divide it into parts as in skills such as diving and pole vaulting.

During this first stage you should be aware that your progress will not be steady. You will seem to learn a great deal in a short time and then progress very little for a while. These plateaus need not discourage you if you understand that your Control System is forming habits that will enable you to take another forward leap in the future.

Another rule to remember during your learning period: Practice form instead of trying for maximum performance. If you try to put the shot as far as you can, or hit the ball as hard as you can, you have less chance of using correct form. That causes you to develop faults. If you try for form first, maximum performance will come more surely later on. Even during early competition, you should practice technique.

When trying to teach your Control System, give it a positive direction, not a negative. Your Control System does not understand negatives. During a golf drive, avoid saying, "Don't hold your right elbow against your side." Instead, say "Hold your right elbow about an inch from your side."

Your transition from the first stage to the second stage may not be noticeable. Suddenly, you are drilling to perfect a skill you know how to do. If you are a bowler, you can hit the number one pin every time by the time you finish the first stage. Now, in the second stage, you want to improve your aim so that you can hit within an inch of your target. The first stage is learning fundamentals; the second stage is drill. Ideally, you will continue drilling until you are so good that further progress seems unlikely; then you need drill only enough to maintain your skill. In actuality, you will have neither the time nor the inclination to drill so much.

You can reduce the time necessary for drilling by intense concentration. That does not mean you tense your muscles and force every movement. It means you concentrate on making the best possible movement each time. For example, if you are practicing passing a football, you should not be content every time your receiver catches the ball. You should strive for absolute accuracy, to within a foot or so of the best target, rather than within the two-yard range that can be caught.

Another way to reduce drilling time is to find ways of practicing more frequently. For example, a tennis player might hit a forehand drive as much as 150 times in an hour-and-a-half match. If he wanted to practice his forehand drive he could rally with another player and hit that many forehands in half an hour. But if he used a backboard he could hit 150 forehands in ten minutes.

You can learn a skill faster and more completely if you concentrate on it alone for short periods of time. If you play golf for enough years you may gradually learn something about blasting out of a sand trap. But one top woman golfer practiced nothing else for several hours and became so proficient that her opponents preferred to see her on the edge of the green than in the trap.

This concentration on each skill for a short time will help keep up your interest. Variety is the spice of life.

You will undoubtedly start playing long before your skills have been perfected, so the third stage will overlap the second. In this third stage you practice using your skills in a competitive situation.

The most common way to do this, of course, is to play. But, as pointed out above, some of your skills may not be used often enough to give you practice.

The best way to practice competitive use of your skills is to set up situations. A coach will do this in team sports and sometimes in individual sports. In tennis, for example, one player can practice forehands down the line while the other player practices backhands down the line.

You can set up situations for yourself so that you can practice while playing. If you value your practice more highly than winning a practice match, you can hit all your backhands down the line and even set up shots to your backhand.

The maximum practice is comparable to a discus thrower

throwing for distance many times in practice, or a high jumper jumping for height. A few years ago, coaches did not permit athletes to try their hardest in practice; instead they practiced form. In other words, they overlooked the third stage. It is as if a hockey player always practiced shooting into a net where there was no goalie.

If your skill breaks down under the pressure of competition, you must go back to stage two and do more drill until your Control System will produce that movement correctly under any circumstances. You may have to go back to stage one and emphasize learning again.

This should be done with an absence of pressure, because then your Control System has no interference; it reproduces the desired movement the same each time. Only when fear causes you to have negative thoughts of failure will your Control System follow your conscious mind and give you a faulty movement.

When you begin to practice your skills in competitive situations and in actual competition, you will probably find some faults in your form. If the fault is because you failed to learn part of your movement correctly, you should go back to the beginning and learn it. If the fault is because you have not drilled enough to "groove" your skill, you should do more drilling.

The worst thing you can do is continue playing and make the best of your fault. If you do that you will be like the sixty-year-old golfer who always slices to the middle of the fairway: You will get along, but your future will be limited.

Do not forget the place of imagination in your practice. You can send messages to your Control System by imagining correct form and winning style. You should do a little of this every day, perhaps when you are most relaxed. You can prepare yourself for future emergencies by imagining all possible situations and yourself making the movements necessary to solve them.

Your training program should now contain a list of drills to practice, methods of practicing for simulated competition, and the number of times you should practice each one. If you keep a record of your practice, you can see at a glance which skills you are neglecting. You should even grade yourself on your progress.

Many athletes do a minimum of practice with the team and then wonder why another athlete makes such amazing improvement. Jack Davis was almost mediocre as a freshman high hurdler, with an unofficial best time of 14.6. After working four hours a day, he won the national collegiate championships as a sophomore in 13.7.

Practice does not always make perfect, but if properly done it will bring you as close to perfection as you can get. And *nobody* ever approached perfection *without* practice.

In summary, you learn to do by doing. That means you should practice your *whole* sport. But you must work up to it gradually, while making certain you learn each *part* correctly. Otherwise it would be like trying to build a car before you learned to build an engine, gears, and wheels.

C H A P T E R • I V

Mental Control

A subtitle for this section could be, "How to Use Your Head."

When your body is in the best possible condition and you have learned all the necessary skills, you should be ready to play your best, but that is not always the case. Many a fine athlete, well prepared, has failed in competition because he did not use his head.

The broad term "Mental Control" covers three activities that can make full use of your physical capabilities:

A. PLANS

If you go into competition without a plan, it is like starting on an auto trip without a map: You may get lost.

In the heat of competition you will not have the time and the emotional serenity to stand off and take an objective look at what is happening. You will not always be able to make a quick and accurate decision. And the more tired you become, the more this is true.

For that reason, you need a plan—a map or a blueprint—that will keep your Control System directed toward your goal.

Your Control System is an automatic mechanism that will do what you tell it to do. But if you are in doubt, if you are afraid and visualize defeat, if you keep changing your plan—your Control System will become confused and will not function in a calm and certain way.

You can fix your Control System on the best possible path by correct planning, and it will continue until you make a conscious decision to change it.

Your first step in making a plan is to collect information. Learn all you can about your opponents, the site of competition, and yourself.

Information about yourself may not be as easy as you think, especially near the beginning of your career. A tennis player, for example, should have an idea of his percentage chance to make each shot; in certain situations he should use a shot giving him a 90 percent chance and his opponent 50 percent instead of one that gives his opponent no chance at all but gives himself only a 40 percent chance of making it. The tennis player should also know how these percentages change *for him* when he begins to tire.

Information about the site of competition differs for each sport. The site is standard and seldom varies in sports such as billiards, bowling, and gymnastics, but you would be extremely foolish to begin play in a golf tournament without examining the course.

A race driver often walks the entire track to find anything that might affect his driving. Charley Greene, a world-record sprinter, made a habit of walking down the track to the finish line to be sure he did not stop running at the wrong line.

Anything out of the ordinary about the surface or the lighting can call for a difference in planning.

Information about your opponent, of course, is the most important and the most difficult to obtain. If you have played against him before it is easy if you really thought it out, and you should have a report in your training diary. If you have watched him play you have learned something, but if you have never seen him, your information will probably be insufficient.

Professional teams and some well-organized amateur teams have full scouting reports on their opponents. A baseball pitcher goes over each batter in the opposing lineup, reviewing his strengths and his weaknesses. But you will not have this advantage at first.

You can sometimes learn something from newspaper reports, or you might learn from someone who has seen your opponent play. As a last resort, you might make some deductions while watching your opponent during his warmup in sports such as tennis and basketball.

After you have collected as much information as you can, you begin to make your basic plan. That may seem complicated because of the number of possibilities you must consider, but it is actually fairly simple if you go about it in a positive manner.

You should have a general plan already, one that fits your own capabilities, using your strengths and compensating for your weaknesses. For example, a distance runner knows the ideal pace he can run for his best time.

When you make your plan, you retain as much of your general, basic plan as possible, changing it only to fit the new situation imposed by the site and your opposition.

In addition to this plan, you should have alternate plans to put into effect when necessary. A change in plans may be necessary if the weather changes, if your opponent changes tactics, or if your skills fail because of fatigue or any other reason.

This set of plans should cover every possible situation. Then you begin to imagine yourself in all those situations, and you send pictures of a successful plan for each one of them to your Control System. When the time comes, you will be prepared.

An outstanding example of the value of an alternate plan took place in the 1968 Olympic Games at Mexico City. Defending discus champion Al Oerter was not supposed to win, and he was given a chance for a medal only because of his outstanding record for coming through in tough competition. Oerter said:

"Once in the Olympic Village you can't improve on your strength or speed. The only thing still possible is to improve your mental attitude. In the weeks before an Olympic competition, I mentally simulate every conceivable situation for each throw. For example, I imagine I'm in eighth place, it's my fifth throw, and it's pouring rain. What do I do? An inexperienced thrower might panic or be thinking, 'Gees, I hope I don't fall down.' I know ahead of time what I will do under every condition."

A light rain began to fall soon after the throwers started to warm up. The others were frustrated, and they sat around the dressing room waiting and fretting. But Oerter kept walking back and forth for 25 minutes, keeping himself warm. They had to throw without proper warmup, but Oerter made the three best throws of his life and won the gold medal.

Part of your plan should include conservation of your strength and energy. In many sports, such as tennis, basketball, soccer, cycling, the decathlon, and the endurance races, the winner is often the one who handles fatigue best. You can avoid anaerobic fatigue by pacing yourself properly, resting as much as possible between plays, and making a wise choice of tactics. You can avoid fatigue from glycogen deficiency by tactics that shorten the contest, by getting off your feet whenever possible, and by consuming glucose throughout the competition.

For example, in a five-set tennis match lasting more than three hours, the player who runs out of glycogen first will lose. You can avoid that by sitting down each time you change sides, by playing a harder-hitting game that avoids long rallies, and by sipping a salt-and-glucose solution at each change.

B. EMOTIONAL CONTROL

It is well known that the "fired-up" football team often upsets the cool, confident favorite.

It is also well known that excitement or fear can produce enough tension to ruin skills and cause defeat.

Your problem is to "fire-up" enough to get the best out of yourself and yet remain calm enough to relax all unnecessary muscles and move gracefully and efficiently.

To do your best you must try as hard as you can, and yet your most skillful movements are relaxed and graceful.

How can you manage these apparently opposite aims?

That question is the most important one of all when you

consider the subject of competitive ability. To answer it requires careful consideration of several facts. First, consider what happens to you when you are fired-up, which simply means that you are excited and *want* to compete and win. It starts with a secretion of adrenaline, which gives you an almost sick feeling of butterflies in your stomach and stimulates your muscles and organs into readiness for physical exertion. Many top-grade athletes "psych" themselves into this condition by various methods, such as imagining or talking about competition and victory. Coaches do the same thing with pep talks. The cheering of a crowd stirs an athlete to this state.

When you are in this excited state, several benefits are noted. The most obvious is that you "hustle." A basketball player goes after the ball like a wild man, and sometimes he gets it. If he stood back and watched, he would never get the ball in that situation. Hustle can win games, but it is possible for you to hustle in a calm, purposeful manner.

Another benefit you receive from excitement is, apparently, added strength. Many stories are told about people who lifted objects during the excitement of emergencies that later on they could not budge. The explanation for this is not known, but part of the answer may have to do with a lack of inhibitions. You do not stop and think, "This is impossible." You go ahead and try it because it is so important, and sometimes miracles seem to happen.

That sort of miracle does not take place in sports, probably because an athlete is already trained to use his strength. If your skill is developed properly, you cannot add to its power by being emotional instead of relatively calm.

Another benefit from excitement is that it masks fatigue so that you can ignore it and continue to compete. That is an important benefit, but an excited feeling at the start of a football game cannot mask your fatigue near the end, so your own drive must be supplied when it is useful.

Although physiologists admit these benefits of excitement, they also point out that excitement can reduce skill and accuracy.

From these facts you can see that you can make yourself do anything that a state of excitement can make you do. In addition, if you remain calm you will retain more of your skill.

If that is true, why do athletes try to fire up? The answer is that its value depends upon the sport, and some athletes are using it in the wrong sport. Its greatest value is in added strength and hustle and in masking fatigue. In a sport such as football those benefits are of great value while most of the play requires relatively little accuracy. For those reasons, football teams benefit greatly from being fired up.

On the other hand, accuracy sports such as billiards or golf require little of the benefits of excitement, and it can cause loss of accuracy.

The conclusion, then, is that the amount of firing up you do depends upon the sport and even upon the specific requirements of a particular moment.

You should develop your own methods of stimulating yourself to greater effort. A racehorse has a jockey to apply the whip when he needs this added emotional stimulus. Most teams have a coach and a rooting section. But in many situations you are all alone; you must be able to stimulate yourself.

This "whip" can be anything that works. Some athletes talk to themselves, silently or aloud. Sometimes they criticize themselves too much; that is not the best kind of stimulus, for it presents the Control System with a negative picture. A far better type of self-help is a positive thought about the benefits you will gain if you try your best. Imagine yourself winning, imagine the approval of your friends, imagine your name in headlines, imagine all the possible rewards—anything that will help you hustle, and use those stimulants when you need them.

Next, consider what happens when you are calm and relaxed.

When you are relaxed, experts say, you do not feel the emotions of fear, worry, and anxiety. And fear causes tension. It is a vicious circle, with each increasing the other. The inhibitions of fear can cause you to freeze completely, and to a lesser extent they can cause loss of skill and accuracy.

Fear is part of the reason for "purpose tremor," a medical

term describing the way your hand trembles when you try to thread a needle or balance a cup of coffee while walking across a room. The tremor is the result of tension, which is the result of trying to guide your Control System with conscious effort.

The best handwriting or drawing is done with a quick, light stroke. A slow, intense effort usually results in crabbed lines that are not where you wanted them. Any movement is more skillful and accurate if it is relaxed and easy.

Many people think they are being more careful and therefore more accurate by slowing their movement and using more muscles to control it. That is the only way you can do it at first, but once your Control System has learned the skill, you must leave it alone. You must tell it what you want it to do, but it can do it better than you can with your conscious mind.

If you do not believe that, try playing the piano or typing while thinking out each finger position. Or, for that matter, try something simple, such as walking or picking up a pencil. If you plan your movements one at a time and try to control them with your conscious mind the result is confusion.

The time to use your conscious mind is when you are deciding whether to shoot or pass off, whether to hit down the line or crosscourt, whether to sidestep or plunge. Once you have made the decision, let your Control System guide your nerves and muscles. It will do the best possible job. Never, *never*, NEVER try to communicate with your Control System in the midst of a movement.

In tennis, for example, you are in communication as long as you are watching the ball, but once your swing starts, let it go. If you try to think through your stroke, tension will result. Extra muscles will tighten, and you will add something that does not belong to your stroke. In other words, you will choke. You might punch too hard, or stop your follow-through, or rotate your wrist, or tilt your racket face, or lift your racket, or you might do several of them. The best strokes are made without thinking. You do not feel much of anything in a good stroke, because the correct movement is unconscious.

Calmness and relaxation can be destroyed by negative thoughts. Like the golfer who fears a hook and then promptly hooks, you can give your Control System the wrong picture by fearing a mistake.

It does no good to tell yourself, "I won't fear anything." All you can do is fill your mind with positive thoughts so that there is no room for fear.

Instead of dreading the hook out of bounds, which will cost you two strokes, think of what causes a hook. Feel yourself swinging the club with your right elbow away from your body. Imagine the ball sailing straight down the fairway. Give your Control System nothing but positive pictures of the result you want.

Here is a good example of the power of positive thinking: Tom Watson stood on a mound at the edge of the 17th green at Pebble Beach, facing a treacherous situation. He was tied with Jack Nicklaus in the 1982 U.S. Open, and he needed a par to remain in contention on the last hole. His ball was in tall grass and the hole was on a slope of the slick green. It seemed impossible to stop the ball close enough to the hole to make a par. Any shot strong enough to get out of the rough would surely send the ball rolling far past the cup. Watching on television near the 18th, Nicklaus felt sure Watson would need a birdie on the 18th to tie him.

Watson's caddie said, "Get it close."

That was the problem: Stop the ball close enough to sink the putt. The natural feeling of most people, including many professional golfers, would be one of despair. "Here I am, about to blow it all," they'd think.

But Tom Watson is not like most of us. He thinks positively, not negatively. He told his caddie, "I'm going to sink it."

He took his stance, studied the situation once more, and swung delicately. The ball popped up, over the grass, onto the green, and rolled into the cup!

Nicklaus was shocked. Bill Rogers, playing with Watson,

called it, "A thousand to one shot." Some people said, "Watson is the luckiest golfer alive."

Watson does seem to be lucky, but it happens too often to be luck all the time. He is highly skilled, but so are many other golfers. The difference is in Watson's attitude. Where most golfers would be tense with negative thoughts about their bad situation, Watson thinks, "I'm going to sink it." That gives him two advantages over his opponents.

First, it gives him an aiming point. He visualizes the ball going into the cup. Others visualize the ball stopping within a few feet of the cup. They hit their target, and Watson sometimes hits his.

Second, Watson does not block his Control System. He has skills, from long hours of practice, and he allows his Control System to use those skills. Others, through fear and pessimism, tighten their muscles, and their Control System cannot operate efficiently. They make mistakes.

This relaxation that allows Watson to be "lucky" so often is a combination of physical and mental techniques. You can learn to relax physically, but it will not work if your mind is full of fear or negative thoughts. When you have a reasonable skill, the ball will go close to where you expect it to go. If you think, "Out of bounds," you are more likely to knock it out of bounds than if you think, "Down the middle."

Another pro, practicing that same "miracle" shot of Watson's, would soon hit one into the cup. He could not do it all the time, nor could Watson, but he could do it. Then, after he had done it, if he bet his entire fortune on the next shot, he would probably be so tense that he would not come close.

Confidence allows your Control System to use whatever skills you have to the best of your ability. Confidence and tension are opposites. Confidence gives you a positive attitude, whereas a negative attitude gives you tension. And a positive attitude helps create confidence.

It is not easy to think positively instead of negatively. You must practice it. A lot of athletes *never* try, but you can make progress if you *always* try. You must do some philosophizing with yourself, long before you are in a crucial competition.

The first philosophical thought you should always remember is that this is sport. You are in it for health and fun as well as for victories. Never let it seem so important that it controls you.

Remember that for every winner there is at least one loser. In the Boston Marathon there are thousands of losers. If you think nothing is important except victory, you need a psychiatrist instead of a coach. Almost everybody loses at one time or another. The greatest batter is out more often than he is safe. Losing is not a tragedy; it is a fact of life in the sports world. Your pride should come from doing your best, not solely from winning. If you break your personal record for the mile by five seconds, take pride in that; don't mope because another runner ran even faster.

If you take that attitude of enjoying competition, of enjoying your progress, of enjoying whatever glory comes your way, you will not only enjoy your sport instead of coming to hate competition, but you will also perform better because of your positive attitude.

Anytime you can say, "I have everything to gain and nothing to lose," you have a chance of doing your best. Anytime your main thought is fear of defeat, you will not perform as well.

Think of yourself as a machine. Your body can perform certain skills under the guidance of your Control System. Under any preplanned program, your Control System works perfectly in answer to commands from your conscious mind. If you give the right commands, your machine will operate at its best. But if you foul the machinery with confusing, negative commands, it will not operate correctly.

That means your Control System should receive only carefully calculated commands without emotion. Thus, the best emotional control is no emotion at all. The best commander is a calm mind. You can teach your Control System to relax all your unused muscles while only your needed muscles are active.

It may be hard to believe, but think about biofeedback for a moment. It has been proven that with biofeedback methods, people can exercise some control over their involuntary organs, and that is more difficult than controlling the muscles.

You can relax during stressful situations if you train yourself. Start by learning "The Relaxation Response" (from the book by Dr. Herbert Benson, Associate Professor of Medicine at Harvard University). His experiments at Harvard in the early 1960's proved the ability of transcendental meditation to lower high blood pressure and other involuntary functions while increasing alpha waves. Dr. Benson asserts that you can teach yourself this simple relaxation response:

1. Sit comfortably in a quiet place for about twenty minutes.
2. Concentrate so as to keep your mind free of other disturbances. You can use a word as in T.M. or you can concentrate on belly breathing as in yoga. Dr. Benson advises using any simple word such as "one."
3. Be passive. If other thoughts enter, return to your concentration. Your goal is to stop thinking.

When you have learned this passive relaxation you can begin to use it anywhere, before a contest or even between plays, but your greatest need is for relaxation while you are playing.

That calls for muscular relaxation. Your first step is to recognize the difference between relaxed muscles and tense muscles. Start by clenching your fists and then let them relax as much as you can. Go through your whole body, first tensing a muscle or set of muscles, then relaxing. When you are sure you have relaxed as much as possible, tell yourself, "This is the way I want this muscle to feel when I am not using it." Your goal is to become aware of unwanted muscular tension so that your Control System knows you want relaxation.

When you can recognize the difference between muscular tension and relaxation, your next step is to practice relaxing various muscles consciously. Your goal is to recognize tension wherever it occurs and be able to relax immediately, as if you pushed a button marked "Off."

This may take some time, but you should soon become aware of your tension, and your awareness makes relaxation possible. Even a tension habit of many years can be improved in a few days and conquered in a few months.

Your third step is to practice relaxation while in action. Start with one skill, such as shooting a basket. Practice using all the necessary muscles while relaxing all others. You may discover some bad habits, but you can overcome them if you isolate your movement and concentrate on finding and destroying tension.

You may have to practice each skill for some time to erase bad habits, and you may have trouble repeating your relaxation during the heat of competition, but you will improve if you try.

Your last step is to relax automatically, without the need for conscious effort. If you can learn to relax consciously, you can learn to do it automatically. Your Control System will take over and relax unneeded muscles if you tell it strongly enough. Keep working at it, and sooner or later it will become automatic.

Then all you need do is check it once in a while to make sure it is working well and keep issuing orders to your Control System in practice.

You can learn to make a habit of relaxing.

C. CONCENTRATION

Concentration means exclusive attention. Exclusive means that your mind is on only one thing at a time. But to be of value, your concentration must be on the *right* thing.

The object of your concentration changes with the sport and the immediate situation in that sport. In most sports you have a target—usually a ball or an opponent—and your eyes and your entire attention should be on that target while you are trying to reach it.

But then your concentration changes. In tennis, you stop concentrating on the ball and concentrate on reaching the proper position after a shot or pass. In football, after you hit your target—an opponent—you concentrate on maintaining contact during your charge.

After a point ends, in tennis, you do not concentrate on either your opponent or the ball. You concentrate on other important goals. If you think through the action of your sport, you will be able to decide where your concentration should be at all times:

- During your attempt to reach a target, concentrate on the target. That means you watch the ball until you hit it. If the ball is to be propelled—as in basketball, bowling, shuffleboard, pitching, passing, soccer, hockey, or water polo—concentrate on where you want it to go. If your target is an opponent—as in football, boxing, fencing, or wrestling—concentrate on the part of him you want to reach. That is your only concentration during such a movement.
- As soon as you have finished that movement, concentrate on preparation for the next one. In some sports this means try to anticipate your opponent. In a few sports—such as golf, billiards, archery, and bowling—that is not necessary because your opponent is not playing your ball. In boxing and fencing it is the very essence of the sport.

If you concentrate on your opponent before he makes his move, you can anticipate his direction. That is not the same as guessing. When you guess, you have an even chance of being right, but with good anticipation you can be right most of the time.

In tennis, for example, your opponent's feet and body position and the way he begins his stroke all give you clues as to where the ball will go. If you concentrate on anticipating his direction, you will often be able to start before you actually see the ball going in that direction.

- Between plays, concentrate on sending positive pictures and commands to your Control System. This was discussed under emotional control, but it requires a conscious effort on your part to keep the right messages flowing. Form the habit of doing it before each movement.

• Remind yourself to hustle. As discussed previously, you can prod yourself into hustling through nonemotional thoughts. Again, that requires a conscious effort, and it should be a part of the image you send to your Control System between play.

• Concentrate on tactics as often as necessary. In most sports you have time to think between important action. In addition to the two emotional-control measures above, you should give a few seconds of your concentration to tactics.

• You are operating along the lines of your general plan, but you need to think about how well it is working and consider any necessary changes. Is your opponent surprising you in a way that calls for a change of tactics? Is one of your skills better or worse than you expected? Give it your attention for a moment between plays.

• Critique. All your other spare moments, which range from a few seconds up to the fifteen minutes between halves, should be spent in a concentrated critique of your overall performance.

This criticism should not be a negative denunciation of all your mistakes, but a positive search for ways to improve. It includes all the points discussed above plus a check of your physical condition and a check of your skills.

In order to cover all points, you need to memorize a checklist and go over it again and again. Athletes in competition tend to turn off much of their brain power; such a checklist will help your brain function under difficulties.

The list should be simple:

Am I watching the ball?
Am I hustling?
Am I sending only positive pictures to my Control System?
Am I using the right tactics?
Am I strong enough to keep going to the end?
Am I making full use of each of my skills?

The next-to-last question is simply a means of checking your endurance to be sure you do everything necessary. You need a sublist of aids to endurance, as discussed previously.

The last question, about your skills, may require some time to answer in a complicated sport such as tennis. For example, your sublist would examine each stroke in turn. Is your forehand going deep enough? Fast enough? To the corner? This sort of review while changing sides will keep you concentrating on positive thoughts that will do you some good.

Now you know what it means to *concentrate*. An athlete who stands up under pressure and plays his best game even when he is losing can take more pride in himself than if he wins an easy victory based upon superior ability. That is the real value of sport.

SUMMARY

Success in sports is a combination of several qualities:

- Direction of natural ability into the right sport. Choose your sport after careful consideration of your size, strength, speed, quickness, endurance, agility, accuracy, adaptability, and cooperation.
- A training plan that guides you through all the steps. Plan for the amount of strength, speed, and endurance you need. Plan for learning skills. Keep a training diary to record your progress.
- Conditioning for maximum useful strength, speed, and endurance. Develop the general and special strength you need by weight training. Develop the speed you need by learning to start fast and accelerate fast. Learn correct technique first, *then* make it a reflex action. Do aerobic training for general endurance. Do some extra long training to develop your glycogen reserves. Eat the necessary raw materials.
- Health. Keep clean and avoid stress, germs, and harmful foreign material. Take proper care of injuries. Eat a well-balanced diet plus supplements.

- Correct skills. Use your Control System by showing it the correct goals and then letting it do the work.
- Enough desire to do the necessary practice. If you practice correctly, the more you practice, the better you will be. Your success depends upon how hard you try.
- Concentration on correct mental control. Plan for all possible situations. Avoid emotions when possible. Concentrate on calmly giving positive orders to your Control System. Memorize a checklist to remind you to concentrate even in the heat of battle.